Crimes Worse
Than Death

Crimes Worse

Than Death

by

Kate Shanahan

Attic Press
Dublin

First Published in Ireland in 1992 by
Attic Press
4 Upper Mount Street
Dublin 2

British Library Cataloguing in Publication Data
Shanahan, Kate
Crimes Worse Than Death: How Violence is Terrorising Women
I. Title
364.1

ISBN 1-855940-531

The publisher acknowledges with thanks E J Murray and the Photographic Society of Ireland.

Cover Design: Conor Gallagher
Origination: Sinéad Bevan, Attic Press
Printing: The Guernsey Press Ltd

For my parents
Bridie and Tom Shanahan
and
to the memory of a dear friend
Derek Dunne

Acknowledgements

The author wishes to thank the following people for their help: Hugh Lambert, Eoghan Corry, John Garvey, Seán Mannion, Louise Ní Chriodháin and Sarah O'Hara of *The Irish Press*, Mary Carr *Evening Herald*, Monica O'Connor, Róisín McDermott, Ursula Barry, Mary Crilly, Anne Kiely, Joan White, Cris Mulvey, Anne Taylor, Pauline Conroy Jackson, Jerry Shanahan, Lavinia Kerwick, Olive Braiden, Maeve Lewis, Grace O'Malley, Ronit Lentin, Susan Russell, Fran Carey, Noreen Byrne, Margaret Tynan, Dorothy Morrisey, Ruth Torode, Geraldine McLoughlin, Kieran McGrath for kindly allowing me access to his research papers, Kathleen Murray for sharing with me her thesis on rape and the law, Gráinne Healy and everyone at Attic Press, and all of the anonymous survivors who told their stories. Most of all I would like to thank Johnjoe for his love and support.

ABOUT THE AUTHOR

Kate Shanahan is a journalist and columnist with *The Irish Press* newspaper. She holds a BA in Politics from the University of Limerick and an M Phil in Women's Studies from Trinity College Dublin. In 1988 she received an A T Cross journalism award for news features with *Hot Press* magazine.

Contents

Introduction

The community worker who tells the following story is not the kind of woman who is easily shocked, but she admits that it is one of the most disturbing things she has heard in years. A group of young boys were discussing joy-riding (stealing cars and driving them very fast) and its effects. 'There's no point in doing cars anymore,' one of them said sagely, 'when you can do a rape and get away with it.' They had realised, the community worker said, that given both their age and what can happen in a court case, the chances of receiving a custodial sentence in a rape case were minimal.

Many Irish women are concerned about the attitude Irish society is taking towards violence against women. It can be argued that society in general is more violent and many citizens now feel themselves to be at risk both in their homes and on the streets. What is different about sexual violence or violence within the family is that it is the one type of violence where the victim almost always has to prove that she did not in any way contribute to what happened.

In their reading of newspaper accounts of court cases, women have begun to wonder if violence against them is increasing, and if it is becoming more severe. They have also begun to question the decisions being made in court cases, particularly where the defendant pleads guilty and is given a suspended or short sentence. There is a feeling abroad that the courts, in distinguishing between 'bad' and 'really bad' assaults, have failed to take into account the long-term effects sexual violence has on all its victims. Women have begun to ask themselves why this is happening now, and if there has been an increase in the reporting of violent crimes against women, or an increase in the incidence of such crimes. Women have begun to wonder if the sentencing policy now in operation is a function of the overall treatment of and attitudes towards women in Irish society.

This book has been written because violence and the fear of it affects each and every woman in our daily lives. Many people asked me if, having researched this book, I would take a case to court, were I attacked. What I am certain of is that I would not have a trusting attitude towards the judicial system in this country. I would expect to encounter hostility and disbelief and I would not be as sure as I once was, of gaining vindication in an Irish court.

The other most frequently asked question relates to the women that I interviewed. What were they like, women wanted to know. What was Lavinina Kerwick like? What were the women who had been battered like? Were the rape victims really in a bad way? It is the intention of this book to tell these women's stories. They are no different from any other Irish woman I've met. What I did discover is the extraordinary resilience, bravery and courage of the women of this country.

The kindness of women to each other is overwhelming. It is the key feature in every woman's desperate plight and situation. For the woman who arrived at a refuge late at night, having hitched 200 miles with two children under five in the middle of winter, her face battered and bloody, kindness came in the form of a woman, a refugee in the packed shelter who gave up her bed to the new arrival. 'I know what it's like,' she told the exhausted woman, 'to travel a long distance with small children.'

This story is not an uncommon one and it illustrates that for every woman who tells herself that violence does not really happen and that the victim must have contributed in some way to her own fate, there are other women who will say, 'Yes I believe you.' This book is about belief, it is about the woman's story which may be changed, distorted and taken from her when she goes to court, but one which she knows is the truth, the truth as it is experienced by Irish women.

In dealing with the background to violence, various experts outline the problems they have encountered. Such problems are at the core of what this book sets out to do: to express and analyse the fears of Irish women and to ask why nothing is being done to allay those fears. The Lavinia Kerwick case focussed the spotlight on the issue of violence in Irish society. The question is why was Lavinia Kerwick treated in the way she was by the courts? Is her treatment markedly different to that which other women victims of violence experience daily? Domestic violence, rape, sexual assault and child sexual abuse are all examined because they are the 'flash-points' where violence most affects the lives of women and children.

No society can allow its legal system to become alienated from at least half of its citizenry, nor can it at the same time expect the law to solve what are essentially social problems. Finding themselves caught between governmental indifference and legal inadequacy, Irish women are now demanding that their concerns be heard. The survivors of assault find it very difficult to speak about what has happened to them. The women who broke their silence to be interviewed for this book all did so with one proviso: they wanted Irish society to change so that no other woman would have to be put through the same ordeal they had suffered.

As one woman who phoned a radio chat show while the controversy over the Lavinia Kerwick case raged said, 'There are crimes worse than death.' And so the idea for giving a voice to the views of women on the subject of violence against women was born, and a title chosen.

Kate Shanahan

Prologue

Every week the nun would read out loud from her copy of the book *Lives of the Saints*. Sometimes if we were particularly good she would read out our favourite extract, the story of Maria Goretti. We would listen again to the by now familiar tale: the young widow and her daughter Maria who worked for a wealthy Italian farmer, the farmer's evil son who attempted to assault twelve-year-old Maria, Maria's death in order to save herself from dishonour, and finally the happy ending, the penitent attacker who later devotes his life to God. Our nun's innate delicacy when it came to sexual matters prevented her from telling us what Maria's attacker had really tried to do to her. So our innocent nine-year-old minds presumed that he had merely wanted to kiss her.

One day as we absorbed again the details of Maria's martyrdom, a classmate, one of the solid country girls who came by bus each day to our small town school asked an unusual question. Her voice breaking with an emotion that in hindsight was probably anger, she wanted to know why Maria hadn't tried to kill her attacker before he attacked her. The nun was as shocked as we were by the unexpected question. Before she could reply, a hand shot up and another classmate attempted an answer. 'Sister, Sister,' she declared proudly, 'I know why, Sister, because if she hadn't died, then she wouldn't be a saint.'

No further answer was needed.

1

Lavinia Kerwick's story

On 31 December 1990, Lavinia Kerwick's life was irrevocably changed. She had left her home in Kilkenny that evening to attend a disco with her boyfriend of five months, William Conry. There had been no indication from his previous behaviour that the young man whom she had known for a couple of years would that evening rape her. He had never been violent towards her and though he drank, rarely did so in her company. On the way home from the New Year's disco the young couple took a shortcut past the nearby canal, a favourite haunt of courting couples. Some time later a distraught Lavinia rang the doorbell of her home.

Her mother's first question to Lavinia when she answered the door was to ask what had happened to her key. Unable to speak Lavinia brushed past her and told her that she was going to have a bath. When she returned her mother was still waiting up for her. This time her mother wanted to know if there was something wrong and Lavinia told her that she had to have another bath. Her mother's response, that Lavinia had already had a bath, indicated to Lavinia that her mother had instinctively guessed what had happened. 'William forced himself on me,' Lavinia told her mother, unable through embarrassment and shame to explain any further. Following on another bath during which she 'scrubbed and scrubbed until her flesh was raw,' as she herself describes it, Lavinia joined her mother in the kitchen again. Mrs Kerwick's suggestion that they go to hospital or call the police (Gardaí) was met with great resistance by Lavinia. Consumed with fear she held on to the belief that when she woke up the next morning everything would be all right, that it would be as if nothing had really happened.

However, the physical pain she felt on waking reminded her immediately that the events of the previous night *had* really occurred. They had not been a nightmare. Having been contacted by Lavinia's mother, Sergeant John Touhy called to the Kerwick home. On seeing how nervous nineteen-year-old Lavinia was, his immediate instinct was to put an arm protectively on her shoulder. Lavinia shrank back. 'It's okay,' the sergeant told her gently, 'I'm not going to hurt you.' His manner reassured Lavinia sufficiently so that, when asked how she was, she was able to reply, 'It hurts.' When asked if she would go to see a doctor, Lavinia insisted that it would have to be a woman doctor. By that stage the pain had left her feeling very weak, but she was still too frightened to think of making a statement. When she eventually spoke about what had happened it was in the presence of a close girlfriend. The baring of intimate details was made easier by the fact that there was someone there of her own age. Later she repeated the statement in front of a policewoman (ban garda). Lavinia's physical injuries included bruising on her back and chest, internal bruising and internal bleeding.

Although she had made a statement, Lavinia Kerwick was unsure whether she wanted to go through with a prosecution or not. In the next few months as she waited for the case to go to trial she desperately wished that she could pretend that the events of New Year's Eve had not really happened to her. On a number of occasions she thought of trying to cancel it all but was sustained by her innate belief that she could trust the police judgement on the matter.

Two other factors also had a bearing on her decision to stick with the case. Her attacker worked near her home and she saw him every day as did her other sisters. The physical injuries she had sustained also continued to give her trouble; an outbreak of sores led to her being sent by her doctor to Ardkeen Hospital. There she was tested for HIV and herpes. The very idea of being in a Sexually

14

Transmitted Diseases clinic deeply embarrassed her, as did the fact that she was being tested for HIV. In the early weeks after the rape she was convinced that she was pregnant; now she had to deal with the possibility that she had a sexually transmitted disease. In the event her fears were groundless on both counts but they served as a constant reminder of what had happened. No matter how hard she tried it seemed as if her life would never be the same again. Living in a small town she was aware that people knew she had been raped.

Though very nervous on the morning of the court case she was buoyed up by the thought that this would be the end of the waiting and the beginning of some measure of healing. The police who accompanied her from Kilkenny were optimistic and the trauma of having to give evidence was slightly eased by the presence of Sergeant Touhy and the policewoman who had taken her original statement. When the police told Lavinia that the defendant had decided to plead guilty, thus sparing her the need to give evidence, she felt as though a weight had lifted from her shoulders and that her former boyfriend was acknowledging the harm that he had done to her. A number of character witnesses then gave evidence on William Conry's behalf, including a priest, a representative of the local GAA (Gaelic Athletic Association) club and his employer. When the court broke at midday Lavinia and her mother went for lunch sure that they would arrive back afterwards to hear some evidence of Lavinia's physical injuries. The doctor who had originally examined her was in court and there were psychological reports testifying to the victim's mental trauma.

Back in the courtroom the Judge began his summing up and Lavinia overheard Sergeant Touhy telling her mother, 'Get her out. It's going bad. Get her outside.' Lavinia asked the Sergeant what was going on, 'Get her out quickly', he repeated to Lavinia's mother. Lavinia refused to go and as she listened further the full realisation of what the Judge was saying began to sink in. William Conry had pleaded guilty, and taking into account his 'forthright and frank' admission, the fact that the rape was 'not premeditated' and the potential for rehabilitation, Mr Justice Flood had decided to adjourn sentencing the accused for a year. 'You promised me he would go away,' Lavinia said to Sergeant Touhy. 'You promised me he wouldn't get away with it. He's getting away with it.'

Helped outside the courtroom Lavinia kept asking what had gone wrong. 'Did I look like a whore to the Judge?' she begged her mother. 'Was that what happened?' Nearby a group of Spanish students, on a sightseeing trip to the courts, stopped to watch as relatives tried to calm Lavinia. That night back home in Kilkenny she contemplated suicide. The following morning her sister Louise suggested that Lavinia go public with the anger she was feeling. It was Louise who rang the Gerry Ryan show, a national radio station programme, and spoke to the producer. Although they were aware that they had a potential scoop on their hands, the Ryan team contacted their solicitor to ensure that, legally, they could talk to Lavinia. For the first time ever an Irish rape victim was about to give up her anonymity.

On the morning of Thursday 16 July 1992, the national newspapers contained accounts of the trial of William Conry for the rape of Lavinia Kerwick, who was identified only as a nineteen-year-old County Kilkenny woman. As well as giving details about the attack, the newspaper accounts noted Conry's guilty plea and the fact that Justice Fergus Flood had postponed sentencing for a year in order to 'give the defendant a chance'. The only item that marked this particular case from the others which appeared that morning was the brief account of the victim's reaction to the judgement. ' "He's getting away with it," the sobbing victim said as she was led from the court by relatives,' reported Tomás Mac Ruairí in that morning's *The Irish Press*. As they monitored the radio programmes, a routine practice in newspapers, the *Evening Press* staff began to realise that a big story was breaking on the Gerry Ryan radio programme. A phone-in chat and music show, Ryan's programme had been noted for covering controversial issues and appealing to a young audience. In the *Evening Press*, reporter Henry McDonald taped the Lavinia Kerwick interview and within the hour it was a new lead story on the next edition of the *Evening Press*. All over Dublin other newsrooms were also changing their lead stories to take account of the latest developments. 'The rape victim said she felt let down by the entire justice system over the judge's decision,' the *Evening Press* front page story reported. 'She said she was persuaded to go to the police by her mother who believed that "justice would be done". The nineteen-year-old girl told the radio show that she expected that her rapist would go to prison for at least ten years. She described the rape which occurred on New Year's eve as "very violent". She said that the rape lasted more than an hour and caused bruising to her face, eyes and private parts. After her ordeal she felt "guilty and dirty". She said she started taking pills and tranquillisers. She disclosed that the rapist lived in the locality and she is terrified to walk through her own town.'

On the nine o'clock news that evening on the national television channel, Lavinia Kerwick was interviewed again about the trial and her reaction to it. For those who had missed the Gerry Ryan show, seeing Lavinia Kerwick on television brought home to them the historic nature of what was occurring. Not only was a rape victim willing to talk publicly about what had happened to her but she was also allowing her face to be seen. She was now identifiable both to those who knew her in her home town of Kilkenny and to people all over the country. 'I'm appealing to the Minister for Justice,' Lavinia Kerwick said in the course of her television interview, 'to bring this back up for a retrial. I'm begging him from the bottom of my heart, if he has any consideration for girls and for me, and for people who have gone through this, and for people who will probably go through it tonight, if he has anything in him at all, please, I'm begging him to bring it back up.' By the following morning, Friday 17 July, every daily newspaper contained accounts of the television and radio interviews given by Lavinia Kerwick and reaction to her case.

Those critical of Justice Flood's decision were having a clear run, but not for long. The Friday edition of 'Morning Ireland', a current affairs programme, saw the first defence of Justice Flood's decision launched in an interview with one of Ireland's top barristers, Gregory Murphy BL. 'It's not just a case of someone jumping into someone's house, and raping an old woman,' Murphy told his interviewer. These people were only eighteen years of age. They'd known each other for five months; it's a case of things having gone too far. These things happen. There must be a distinction between the cold rapist and something which at the end of the day is just a matter of consent.' Public reaction to the interview with Murphy was swift; the switchboards at the Dublin Rape Crisis Centre and RTE were jammed with calls, the majority of them critical of Murphy's comments.

The most remarkable thing about the Kerwick case and Gregory Murphy's subsequent remarks is the wide range of men and women with a public profile who either chose to defend Lavinia Kerwick or take issue with Murphy. Noirín Greene, equality officer with SIPTU, one of Ireland's largest trade unions, told *The Irish Press* reporter Lóuise Ní Chríodháin, 'Rape is one of the most horrific experiences a woman can undergo, no matter what the circumstances, and the law has to show that it is serious about protecting women in their dealings with any offender, no matter what their background.' Maureen Browne, a member of the government-appointed Second Commission on the Status of Women told the *Evening Press* that she was furious at Mr Murphy's comments. 'I don't think that you can in any way dismiss rape or excuse it on the basis that it may be a so-called "date-rape".' On the same day, *The Irish Independent* newspaper's editorial stated: 'Until the State's right to appeal minimum sentences and guidelines to ensure uniformity are introduced, side by side with improved treatment for offenders, it cannot be claimed with conviction that one of the most serious crimes on the statute book is taken seriously.'

Realising that the story would hold over the weekend, Sunday newspaper editors dispatched journalists to Kilkenny to interview Lavinia Kerwick at home. Writing in *The Sunday Independent* of 19 July one journalist, Molly McAnailly Burke, interviewed barrister Gregory Murphy. It was becoming clear that as well as the human interest angle, a debate was opening up between the legal profession and the public. 'There's a movement afoot,' Murphy told Molly McAnailly Burke, 'which is dangerous, and goes against the civil liberties of those charged with sexual offences. My views have changed since I came to the bar in 1975. In the beginning I was used to defending the ordinary common or garden rapists and by that I mean rapes in which the only issue was consent. Both were usually eighteen years of age, known to each other, and had been to a party or disco where there was a lot of alcohol taken. A girl who knew nothing about sex was late home, her knickers in flitters and she was worried whether she was pregnant or not. The easiest thing was to scream rape. But I've seen a change taking place since then, boys raping old women, the most shocking violence, people cut with knives. What I was trying to do on the radio was distinguish between the two types.' In the same edition of *The Sunday Independent* radio critic Declan Lynch put forward a different viewpoint. 'There is an undercurrent of popular opinion which suggests that certain proponents of feminist thinking are mad. Listening to a couple of horror stories this week, one would have to reach the conclusion that, if they aren't mad, then they should get "mad" immediately.'

By the following week, many more politicians and public figures had taken up the Kerwick case and were demanding changes in sentencing policy. According to those who know him, Mr Justice Fergus Flood was at first genuinely shocked and then angry over the media attention that his decision had generated. Within the law library, the section of the Dublin law courts from which most of the country's barristers practise, opinion was split on the validity of giving William Conry a deferred sentence. Most barristers fully supported the Judge, with a minority of women lawyers feeling that <u>the decision reflected the law's inherent bias against women</u>. Rumours had also begun circulating that the interviews Lavinia Kerwick had been giving to the media were not consistent with her statement in the book of evidence. Mr Justice Flood himself wondered whether any of those now criticising him had read the full text of his decision. Responding to the Justice's statement that he was deeply upset by the media publicity, *The Irish Press* editorial of Thursday 24 July said: 'By all accounts he is a most conscientious member of the bench. But it was his decision to adjourn sentence on the self-confessed rapist in the case, allowing him to go free, that provoked the publicity and caused widespread anger. It would certainly have been more helpful if he had chosen to explain his decision or to comment generally on what has been a matter of national debate rather than threatening the media with contempt of court proceedings for its reporting of the affair. Judges are no longer isolated in remote ivory towers. They live in the same world as the rest of us. Far from seeking to silence the messenger Judges should be paying much more attention to the message.'

Unlike their counterparts in the judiciary, the country's politicians were quick to see which way the wind of public opinion was blowing. Dublin City Council's committee on crime and vandalism urged its chairperson Alderman Gay Mitchell TD to send a letter of support to Lavinia Kerwick. The Minister for Justice Pádraig Flynn agreed to see a deputation from the country's representative body for women, the Council for the Status of Women (CSW). Though ministers do not normally like to be seen to be bowing to public pressure, the consensus of public feeling on the Kerwick case meant that an immediate response was politic. In a statement after his meeting with the CSW, Minister Flynn said that he had ruled out the possibility of mandatory sentencing for rape. 'Those attending the meeting had agreed that this was not the way forward and that there were also methods of dealing with offenders in a non-custodial way.' What the minister had promised the four-woman delegation, comprised of representatives from Women's Aid, the Irish Countrywomen's Association (ICA), the Dublin Rape Crisis Centre, and the executive of the CSW, was that legislation would be introduced to allow the Director of Public Prosecutions (DPP) to appeal against lenient sentencing. This would be done as a matter of priority when the Dáil resumed. Ms Carmel Foley of the CSW told *The Irish Times* that 'she was pleased that the Minister had unequivocally stated that rape was a crime of violence and rejected the idea that it was an act of sexual passion out of control.'

On Tuesday 21 July 700 people gathered at a public demonstration in Kilkenny town to display both their opposition to the general rise in violence against women and the decision in the Kerwick case. The demonstration had been organised by Councillor Margaret Tynan, a former mayor of Kilkenny. 'The laws are in place to deal with violence,' Cllr Tynan said in her address to the demonstration. 'What is wrong is the approach of those administering them.' One Kilkenny woman attending the demonstration told *The Irish Times* reporter Paul O'Neill that she was raped by a relative ten years ago. 'You live with all these things going on inside you; it's you they're destroying.' Her scars had been reopened she said when her sister came to her for help after she was raped while in college in Dublin three years ago. An elderly woman summed up the strong emotions in the crowd when she said why she had come to the demonstration. 'I'm here because we have to do something. Every woman and every man in this country has got to stand up and let them know in those courts and in the government that we are not going to stand for things like this any more. Every woman should feel safe to walk where they want and go out with their boyfriends and be in their homes.' Women politicians echoed the views being expressed by the demonstrators in Kilkenny. Mary Banotti MEP said, 'It's difficult for men to understand the deep sense of humiliation experienced by women who've been raped. Judges are affected by the prejudices of society; they live in a world where most men would say, "Oh, for God's sake, she led him on." ' Former minister Gemma Hussey posed the question. 'If Judges come from the middle-class, are middle-aged to elderly men, mostly catholic educated in single-sex schools with all the attitudes that implies, we need to ask how that group of people is equipped to judge the innermost feelings of a woman who has been raped.'

By Wednesday 22 July Lavinia Kerwick was herself seeking a meeting with the Minister for Justice. Public sympathy for her case had been reinforced by various newspaper reports about her battle with anorexia nervosa, all of which lent an urgency to her request. One week later Lavinia's meeting with Minister Flynn took place at the Department of Justice in Dublin. Accompanied by her mother, Lavinia had arrived by train from her home in Kilkenny. At Heuston railway station television cameras and press photographers jostled for position as the Kerwicks were led to a taxi supplied by the Department of Justice. An anonymous man ran up to Lavinia and presented her with a bouquet of flowers as she got into the taxi. Outside the Department of Justice an official told waiting reporters that a taxi had been ordered to take the Kerwicks home after the meeting which was expected to last about twenty minutes. Lavinia had checked herself out of the local hospital in order to come to see the minister. In fact, the meeting lasted over two hours. 'He told me that he would change the law so that what happened to me would not happen to any other woman in an Irish court,' Lavinia informed the waiting reporters. 'He was very nice; he spoke to me like I was his daughter, and he gave me a lot of good advice.' On 31 July, Lavinia Kerwick gave an interview to *The Star* in which she thanked the people of Ireland for supporting her throughout her ordeal. She said that she would 'never have survived the last few weeks if it had not been for the messages of support. Lavinia said that though her meeting with Justice Minister Pádraig Flynn had given her hope, she was still unsure if she would be alive in a year's time.'

The ~~victim~~ Survivor speaks.

Eight weeks after her rape trial ordeal Lavinia Kerwick sits in the front room of her Kilkenny home, a virtual prisoner, despite the outrage that her case has caused. She now has a telephone and she also has a guard dog in the house, but her family never leave her alone and if she does leave the house she is always accompanied by a family member. The strain has begun to tell on Lavinia's mother whose face seems tired and drawn, even though the whole family has just returned from a holiday in nearby Rosslare. Her first night back in her own home, Lavinia has slept badly and her voice betrays the tiredness she is feeling. Although she has begun to eat small amounts again, her body appears so thin and her movements so slow it's hard to believe, as she says herself that 'I used to have a life before all of this happened.'

Her hopes are now pinned on being able to appeal if a new appeals procedure is set up. 'It's so hard to come to terms with what happened,' she says, 'and perhaps wait for another miscarriage of justice, and then another appeal. I am a human being and I have my rights. They should have been taken into account. I still haven't cried properly over what happened. I will tell people what happened but I won't cry in front of anyone. I see my life five years down the road and I don't see myself ever having a marriage or ever having a future with a man. They say time is a great healer but in my case it's just another day to think about the same thing. I'm sure my family are sick hearing me talk about it, but it angers me to think that he's still out there.'

Reflecting on what has happened to her she is angry on

a number of accounts. The first and most basic is the feeling that as she did not give her evidence the full evidence in the case was not heard in court, neither did the expert witnesses on her behalf take the stand. 'In the end it was as if I didn't exist,' she says. 'I was just a name on a piece of paper. I knew that had I taken the stand I would have been ripped apart. I knew that was what happened to rape victims. It would have been difficult, but at least I'd have got it off my chest.'

The fact that her assailant is free also angers her. 'Even if the Judge had put him away in some kind of care, not even a prison, for say six months. If the Judge had said, "you committed a serious crime; it's worse than murder because the victim is still alive," even if the Judge had said that. What happened was not a judgement and it was unfair on all women who take the decision to go to court.' Though she does not regret the decision to go public on her case – it was, she feels, the only option left to her – she was completely unprepared for the subsequent media attention. In general the media treated her fairly she says. The only rule she herself placed on being interviewed was that male journalists had to sit a certain distance away from her. In the light of what happened to her she now finds it difficult to trust people in general, she says. She wonders about each person who comes to talk to her about her case, what really lies behind their apparently sympathetic facade. 'It's a terribly sad thing to have to say, but I don't trust people any more. I trusted him one thousand and one per cent; now I think, what's trust? The only people I trust are my family and a few close friends.'

(A virgin when she was raped, she was, she says, 'waiting until I met the right person'.) Now the prospect of any kind of close relationship with a man terrifies her. The fact that a single emotion – fear – now dominates her life, also upsets her. 'I feel envious when I see my sister Louise just being able to walk out the door.' Even when the doorbell rings in the course of this interview, she stays rigid, unable to spontaneously answer it. While the fear remains somehow sublimated during the day, the nights are a long catalogue of worrying about every noise as she constantly replays in her mind the events of the past twelve months. What sleep she does get is fitful and dominated by nightmares of being attacked.

Lavinia's close-knit family have been extremely supportive. This, combined with the local community's support for her and the many letters she has received, has in some way helped to ease the pain. Many victims of rape and abuse have written to her, the youngest letter writer being a twelve-year-old girl, also a rape victim, who wrote to her about her own experience of the judicial system. Nothing however can dissipate the feeling of powerlessness that consumes her. 'The anger inside me, I feel as though I'm going to burst with it. No matter where I go I'll always be known for this. People will come up to me and say, "Oh you're Lavinia Kerwick". I'm expected to buck up and get my eating under control, but I hate the body I'm living in. I'm six and a half stone. I'd love to be six. This is my control, the only control I have left. The only thing I have to control is what I eat. Not one person has said you'll get justice because they know that they can't guarantee that. At least with what I eat I can control something.'

Young women like herself are afraid to report it when they have been attacked, Lavinia Kerwick points out, and yet her treatment at the hands of the judicial system could not have encouraged other victims to come forward. 'I felt that day in court as if I'd been raped again.' Her image of what the court would be like was gleaned from watching programmes like the American crime series *Matlock* on television. 'I thought the Judge would be quite close, that I could hear what was going on.' Feeling distant from the procedures going on in front of them is a common experience for victims of assault when they go to court. In Lavinia's case that feeling was exacerbated by the fact that she was face to face with her assailant in a confined space. 'I wish that if I had given evidence it could have been in another room, on video. I think also that there should have been two Judges, and one of them should have been a woman Judge, and that all the evidence should have been brought out in front of the Judge. There should have been a counsellor from a rape crisis centre as well in the court.'

In the aftermath of her case Lavinia asks what the court's definition of justice could possibly have been. She feels betrayed by the legal and political system in general. 'Why should I have had to stand up? What are the people in the Dáil and the courts doing? Why haven't they stood up and said something?' She questions why she or any other woman should have to undergo such violence. 'When I was young there used to be a fella flashing (sexually exposing himself) around here when I was thirteen. That was another type of violence. And now I've been raped. Why do these things happen? After I left the court that day, the Judge said, "She can hold her head high", but he didn't have to go back to Kilkenny. If it had happened to his daughter, how would he have felt?'

Now attending a rape crisis centre for counselling, Lavinia sees herself as perhaps only really having a future outside Kilkenny. Although it will be hard to leave her family and friends, she feels that she can never begin to feel safe until she leaves the town. 'I couldn't stay here for Christmas; it would be very hard,' she says. At the moment she is also preoccupied with trying to get the justice she feels she has been denied and says firmly, 'If I have to go to the Supreme Court, no matter what it costs, I will do it.'

2

The aftermath

The community

On 21 July 1990 a public meeting was held in Kilkenny town to protest at the Judge's decision in the Lavinia Kerwick case and about violence against women in general. Later that evening a seventeen-year-old girl walked to her home through one of the town's main streets. Outside a fast-food restaurant a group of youths who had gathered there after a football match shouted at the young girl as she walked past. At first their jeers and taunts merely embarrassed her, but when they began to throw empty beer cans at her, she became genuinely frightened. She did not recognise any of the youths and was puzzled about the attack, and as the family friend who recounted the incident explained, 'This would not have happened to a boy her age. What is happening when a girl can't walk home in the early evening without being molested?'

Former mayor of Kilkenny Margaret Tynan and local solicitor Anne Kiely, who both serve on the committee which has been formed to set up a rape crisis centre in Kilkenny, have given a lot of thought to the issue of violence in their community. But they both admit that they are unsure of the compelling reason behind the apparent increase in assaults on women. However, they are both agreed that the violence exists and that the women they know are afraid. 'I first became aware of the different types of violence affecting women,' Margaret Tynan says, 'by virtue of the fact that I am a public representative. Because I am the only woman councillor, women were coming to me about issues that they felt uncomfortable talking to my male colleagues about. From a personal point of view, reading newspaper reports and seeing the way the courts were treating violence against women, I felt that this whole issue was not being taken seriously.'

The case of the young American woman who spoke on the Gay Byrne show on national radio, about her brutal experience of rape while living in Kilkenny town also had a profound effect on Margaret Tynan and other Kilkenny women. The decision in the Kerwick case was, as the former mayor sees it, 'the fire which set off the whole feeling here that something had to be done; the decision in the case angered a lot of us.' Solicitor Anne Kiely agrees. 'It was this business that it was date-rape; the double-standard is intolerable. There was no way that he was in danger from her. Why should she have been in danger going out with him? If you know somebody and go out with them, you put yourself in their trust. In certain ways so-called date-rape is worse. In no way should it be acceptable.'

'Rape is violence,' Margaret Tynan interrupts. 'It's inexcusable. When a Judge, for example, says that a defendant was under the influence of drink, that's no justification. We're all responsible for our actions.'

It was the women who approached Margaret Tynan for advice in her capacity as a public representative who convinced her of the need for a rape crisis centre in Kilkenny. But she did have some difficulty in persuading her male colleagues that the level of violence against women warranted immediate action. 'I came across families who had gone through dreadful experiences but who kept it in the family. They did not know where to turn. Some go to the police, but not all. There were people who were suffering quietly at home. In one case a mother had been to a priest about a case of child sexual abuse and was told that these things do not happen, to go home and forget about it.' Anne Kiely believes that 'the fact that a rape crisis centre exists means that people recognise that there is a problem. To the victim it's saying, it's not your fault, you're not going to have to live with this awful secret. It's very important that rape and violence against women are shown as being unacceptable.'

Dealing with the Irish situation she argues that 'violence has gone on at quite a high level in families. We have developed a whole vocabulary for making it less than it is. You know that old phrase, "He used to knock her about a bit." Anyone who deals with family law will know that women make a hell of an effort to keep the family together. When it comes to violence in the home, usually it will have gotten to an extraordinary stage before women go to a solicitor.' As a practising lawyer Anne also feels that there is a lack of cultural understanding when cases of violence against women come before the court. 'A lot of Judges consider that the case in front of them is a once-off case. The case that gets to court is usually a very serious one. What they don't realise is that violence is progressive and a lot of cases of violence don't come before the courts. I don't know if any of them give a thought to the amount of violence that goes on. Or if there is just a casual acceptance of the level of violence. Ireland is a very authoritarian society. If the authorities recognise that violence against women is a serious problem then we can move forward in some way.'

When women like Margaret and Anne talk about fear of being attacked they are also speaking from a personal point of view. They would not, they told me, walk in their own town late at night on any except the main streets, without feeling apprehensive. Both middle-aged, they imagine that younger women must be a great deal more afraid than they are. 'You rarely see a young girl walking on her own at night; usually they are in groups,' Margaret says. 'That's not the way it should be.'

The courts

When barrister Gregory Murphy BL defended Justice Fergus Flood's decision to defer the sentencing of Lavinia Kerwick's rapist for one year, he was expressing a view with which most of the barristers and solicitors in Ireland seem to agree. What Gregory Murphy and his colleagues had not reckoned on, however, was the anger of Irish women in the face of the decision. Eschewing the demand for mandatory sentencing, the legal community argued that imposing this type of sentencing would tie the hands of Judges, and so prevent them from dealing with the particular facts of the case before them. The law is not about revenge, women's groups were told, and to expect it to be so is to completely misunderstand its role in Irish society. Despite these injunctures, four out of five Irish women interviewed for *The Irish Independent*/Irish Marketing Surveys (IMS) poll of 29 August called for mandatory sentencing for rapists. If women were calling for mandatory sentencing then it could only be because they felt that existing sentencing procedures were biased towards defendants, as opposed to victims. To find out whether they are correct in their assumption that sentencing has been too lenient one must look at the type of sentencing passed in the six months prior to *The Irish Independent*/ IMS poll.

Between January and July 1992 the following decisions were handed down in Irish courts in relation to rape, sexual abuse and indecent assaults:

• A teenage baby-sitter who claimed that a six-year-old-girl initiated sex with him was given a three year suspended sentence by the Central Criminal Court for indecently assaulting the child. The case had been adjourned twice and as well as psychiatric counselling the youth involved had the benefit of a probation report which said that the service was satisfied that he had a genuine feeling of remorse.

• A thirty-four-year-old Corkman who sexually assaulted his twelve-year-old niece was jailed for two years by Dublin Circuit Criminal Court. Pleading for leniency the defending barrister said the accused became dependent on alcohol and had spared the victim giving evidence by pleading guilty.

• A Cork businessman who indecently assaulted a schoolgirl after showing her an explicit sex film and sex books was given a suspended three year sentence on each of three charges by Dublin Circuit Criminal Court. Judge Michael Moriarty said that he had decided by only a narrow margin not to jail the man. The defendant had abused his position with the girl in a most squalid way. But he said he had also to take into account the very impressive character evidence offered on his behalf. He was a self-made businessman who offered employment in an economically disadvantaged area. A priest and a member of the St Vincent de Paul spoke on the defendant's behalf.

⚹• A twenty-one-year-old Sligo man who raped a woman while she was unconscious was jailed for six years and ten months by Mr Justice Ronan Keane at the Central Criminal Court. The defendant said that he had drunk about twelve pints of lager on the day of the offence. Passing sentence Mr Justice Keane said he was taking all the positive aspects in the defendant's favour into consideration. Rape was one of the most serious crimes known to the law. The defendant had satisfied himself in a cruel and callous way, with an element of violence.

✗• A father aged forty who admitted fifty charges of sexual and indecent assault on his daughter was jailed for fifteen months by Dublin Circuit Criminal Court. Judge Gerard Buchanan told the man that the sentence was a lenient one for the sake of his family. 'Of all the cases which come before the courts, sentencing in these types of cases presents the greatest problems,' the Judge said. 'There must be punishment for the terrible offences and there must also be support for the families.' The court was told that the defendant had a drink problem and often used violence towards his wife and children.

• A JCB driver was sentenced to five months in jail at Dublin District Court after pleading guilty to exposing himself to a yard full of young primary schoolgirls.

• Two Donegal men who pleaded guilty to having unlawful carnal knowledge with a girl now aged fifteen years were each given a five year suspended sentence by Dublin Circuit Criminal Court. Sentencing the defendants,

Judge O'Connor said that they had committed serious offences but he took into account their previous good characters and guilty pleas.

• A man who pursued a young woman from a Leeson Street nightclub, before attacking and raping her, was sentenced to eight years penal servitude by the Central Criminal Court. Pleading for leniency the defence counsel submitted that the defendant was a man of considerable talent and had won an award as an apprentice butcher. Mr Justice Paul Carney said he considered evidence, that the defendant had drunk fifteen or sixteen pints of beer and taken the drugs hash and ecstasy that night, to be aggravating rather than mitigating factors.

• A man caught sexually assaulting an eighty-year-old woman suffering from Alzheimers disease was jailed for four years by Dublin Circuit Criminal Court. The Judge in the case said that he could not ignore the gravity of an awful attack on a helpless old woman.

• A thirty-four-year-old Waterford city man was jailed for twelve months at Waterford District Court for sexually assaulting a seven-year-old girl. Judge Gerard Buchanan said that he had a duty to the people of Ireland and particularly to the victim of this crime. He said that he had to impose the maximum sentence of twelve months imprisonment. He added that the defendant would be facing a much longer sentence if it had come before a higher court.

• A forty-one-year-old businessman who indecently assaulted his baby-sitter received a three year suspended sentence in the Dublin Circuit Criminal Court. The accused pleaded guilty to sexually molesting the twelve-year-old schoolgirl. A consultant psychiatrist described the accused man to the defending counsel as being 'a chronic alcoholic'. Judge Gerard Buchanan, describing the offences against the young girl as outrageous, imposed a three year suspended sentence and warned the defendant not to contact the victim again.

• A twenty-nine-year-old man who had been sexually

32

abused as a child was jailed for five years when he pleaded guilty at Castlebar Circuit Court to twenty-six charges of indecent assault on two young brothers who had been placed in foster care in his family home.

• A twenty-three-year-old Dublin man who held a garden fork and knife to his elderly neighbour and raped her in her own home was sentenced to ten years penal servitude at the Central Criminal Court. In imposing sentence Mr Justice Kevin Lynch told the accused man that he had violated the constitutional rights of the woman by firstly breaking into her home and then violating her person.

• A twenty-seven-year-old father of three with what a Judge termed a tragic background was sentenced to six years imprisonment at the Central Criminal Court for raping and assaulting a Tallaght woman at her home. Mr Justice Fergus Flood said that he had sympathy for the accused man's family as well as for the rape victim and that he would temper his sentence to leave some light at the end of the tunnel. But he pointed out that this was a serious offence and the accused had terrorised the victim into submission. The woman had been without any blame in the incident even though she 'had been perhaps a little naïve'.

• A sentence of seven years penal servitude was imposed in the Dublin Circuit Criminal Court on a Dublin man who pleaded guilty to the buggery of a mildly mentally retarded man.

• A twenty-four-year-old Cavan man who was given twelve concurrent suspended sentences for buggery was warned by a Judge at Dublin Circuit Criminal Court to curtail his drinking. The unemployed man who had not re-offended since his previous court appearance had however failed to attend AA meetings and continued to drink heavily. The man had admitted eleven charges of buggery on a fourteen-year-old youth and one charge of assault on an eight-year-old boy.

• A twenty-five-year-old rapist who carried out horrific attacks on prostitutes and a widow was given two life sentences in the Central Criminal Court. Mr Justice Carney said that in determining sentence he had to lay aside the usual weight given to guilty pleas by courts and instead consider the protection of all women and in particular prostitutes. He said he had been informed by a psychiatrist that the defendant was a danger to society and likely to re-offend.

• A twenty-five-year-old man received a two year suspended sentence when he admitted two charges of sexual assault against young boys. According to police evidence the two young boys aged eleven and twelve years were forced into acts of masturbation, had their private parts touched and were forced to perform oral sex. The defendant worked as a sports trainer with youngsters. Passing sentence Judge Kirby said that he wished parents would be more vigilant and involved in their children's whereabouts.

• A twenty-one-year-old County Galway man who took an overdose of tablets after admitting he had sexually assaulted his young cousin was sentenced to three years imprisonment by the Central Criminal Court. Passing sentence Ms Justice Susan Denham pointed out that while the accused man's guilty plea had saved the victim the trauma of having to come to court to give evidence, the offence had not been a minor assault. The accused, she said, had betrayed his position of trust and the young girl had subsequently been very frightened of men. Her condition after counselling was improving but there was still a great deal of work to be done. Taking all the elements in the case into account the correct sentence, she concluded, was one of three years.

• A twenty-four-year-old County Kildare man, described by his lawyer as 'not the brightest in the world,' had his sentence for rape adjourned for a year by the Central Criminal Court. However, in freeing him on bail, Mr Justice Fergus Flood warned that any attempt to contact or show any animosity toward the twenty-year-old victim could lead to a minimum jail sentence of eight years. The unemployed man, a neighbour of the injured party, admitted raping the woman on waste ground near their homes.

• A twenty-nine-year-old fisherman was given a five year suspended sentence and ordered to pay £1,500 to a Donegal teenager whom he admitted indecently assaulting in 1988. Passing sentence Judge O'Connor said that he was impressed by the defendant's previous good character. Judge O'Connor said that the Supreme Court on numerous occasions deemed a guilty plea in these cases to be a mitigating factor in imposing sentence. He was therefore going to deal with the matter in a way that might be considered lenient.

• A man was sentenced to three years imprisonment after Dublin Circuit Criminal Court heard his step-daughter had become a born-again christian and had a lock put on her bedroom door following his sexual molestation of her over some years. The girl's mother told the court that her daughter refused to go out with male relations as she used to, and had given up ballet classes and majorettes. The girl had become a born-again christian because her prayers during the years she had been molested had not been answered. At the time of the offences the girl had been six, eight and eleven years old. Imposing concurrent three year sentences in each case Judge Moriarty told the defendant's counsel Mary Ellen Ring BL that should her client continue to make satisfactory progress he would consider a review of the final year of the three year term.

• A youth who sexually assaulted his sixteen-year-old deaf and dumb former girlfriend was sentenced to thirty months detention by Dublin Circuit Criminal Court. Passing sentence Judge Moriarty said he was bewildered by the seeming lack of respect for women in the defendant's family. He noted another member of his family had recently been jailed for eight years for a sex offence. Judge Moriarty said that the youth had behaved scandalously in a sexually contemptuous and intimidating manner, knowing the girl suffered from a disability. But for the prompt appearance of some of the girl's friends the defendant might be facing even more serious charges. Judge Moriarty said that he had no option but to impose a thirty months sentence but would review the matter in March 1993. Pleading for leniency Mr Séamus Breathnach BL told Judge Moriarty that the defendant and the victim were friends and at one time were 'walking out' with each other. They were once next-door neighbours but had now moved. Mr Breathnach described the youth and the young girl as Romeo and Juliet.

The foregoing detailing of sentences handed down in the January-July 1992 period prompts one to make a number of observations. The first and most obvious is that the actual number of cases is quite staggering. If the experience of the rape crisis centres is taken into account, that only a minority of their clients report their assault to the police, then how would the courts deal with it if the current numbers of cases were even doubled? In both the USA and Britain victimisation surveys have been carried out in order to analyse the level of unreported crimes. On average they found that less than half of serious crime comes to the attention of the police. In the USA National Crime surveys are conducted in conjunction with the National Census. In 1986 women in three USA cities were asked whether they had ever been raped or sexually assaulted; eleven per cent said 'yes'.

Whereas in the past, under-reporting of sex assaults could be linked to a victim's fears about how she would be treated by the police and medical authorities, in general facilities for and attitudes towards such victims have improved. The question may well be asked, however, has the legal system in general benefited from our increased knowledge and understanding of the trauma suffered by victims of rape, child abuse and battering? In the sentences handed down between January and July 1992 how did Judges assess the seriousness or otherwise of a particular assault? Are the defendants' psychological reports counterbalanced with those of the victim? If the economic and mental effects on the defendant's family are taken into account, then is the same weight given to the experience of the victim's family?

Pleading guilty is seen to be a mitigating circumstance which saves the victim from having to give evidence. How then does a Judge decide what leeway should be given a defendant if he pleads guilty? Does she or he decide to halve the potential sentence or even drop it to one third of what it might have been? If the sentence given is a two or three years suspended sentence does that mean that the defendant has a choice of three years if he pleads innocent, or of walking free if he pleads guilty?

The mention of alcohol as a mitigating circumstance is an equally interesting phenomenon. Consumption of large amounts of alcohol or having a recognised drink problem would appear to be a positive attribute when defending oneself against a rape or child abuse charge. That same understanding is not extended to cases other than sexual assault where alcohol has been consumed.

The impression given in some of the above judgements is that the effect on the victim only relates to the actual and immediate trauma of the assault, and that there is no need to assess the possible long-term effects. In the case of assaults on children in particular the victim often carries a huge burden of guilt for what has happened. Yet she or he may have to go through a court case in which the offender pleads guilty and still walks free. If the offender lives nearby, which is often the case, the child may continue to perceive him as a frightening threat.

Underlying much of the legal system's attitude to the women and children who are victims of violence are the values by which they judge the relationships between men and women and parents and children. Over the past few years Judges have bemoaned the increased number of rape and incest cases coming before their courts. Could it be that without the benefit of a political will to protect women and children, Judges have begun to apply their own criteria to determine the seriousness of an assault? One could also ask whether Judges have all the relevant information to hand when they make a decision to suspend or defer a sentence. In some north American states, rape has been redefined so that it comes under ordinary assault and battery charges. Since in some rapes the threat of violence is not actually carried out, a minimum sentence could thus be given. To understand why the majority of those interviewed in *The Irish Independent*/IMS survey felt that the courts were not dealing harshly enough with sex offenders Irishwomen's experience of violence and Irish society's response to that violence must be expressed and analysed.

Reading through these court cases a number of obvious messages are being given out both to women and men. Men are being told that if they can explain their behaviour as anything other than their own fault (and alcohol is a front-runner in this field), then Irish courts are ready and willing to listen to them. Women, on the other hand, must wonder what is the point of bringing a complaint to court and what is the level of seriousness now assigned to the crimes committed against women and children in this country. Lawyers conveniently dismiss women's outrage about sentencing as being 'vigilante' style interference in the judicial process. It runs far deeper than that, as they well know. It concerns the role and position of women in Irish society and the value assigned to that role by the institutions of the state. Judging by the attitude of the courts, that value appears to be very low.

3

Pandora's box opens

'It has been an ugly ten days, the air thick with rape, revenge and recrimination. And much detail of the trial was lost in the media-feeding frenzy which followed Lavinia Kerwick's condemnation of the Judge and the sentence.' This is the introduction to an opinion piece written by journalist Sam Smyth in *The Sunday Independent* newspaper on 26 July in which he defended the judgement given by Justice Fergus Flood in the Kerwick case. 'There has also been an element of recrimination,' Smyth wrote, 'perhaps understandable in the victim and her family, but hardly laudable when it is coming from sympathetic pressure groups.' On the same page, journalist and broadcaster Emer O'Kelly outlined her view on the same issue, arguing that 'women want to be able to trust men. And it's becoming increasingly difficult ... . In this year of 1992, in this small island on the edge of Europe, women have been hearing men who have the benefits of all those generations of civilisation, and who also have the inestimable benefit of a supposedly rational education, men who they hope could never be guilty of the crime of rape seeming to excuse those who are guilty of it. Women are hearing men with power and influence refusing to condemn outright the deliberate internal physical violation of another human being's body by means of superior strength.'

The debate as exemplified by O'Kelly and Smyth was one that could be heard all over Ireland in the aftermath of Justice Flood's decision. Viewed in isolation it might appear that what was important were the rights and wrongs of a particular case of which no-one except the parties involved could know the full details. In fact what was occurring was an exploration of an area that had never before been placed under such intense scrutiny: violence against women and Irish society's response to it.

Why did the Kerwick case attract such a high level of interest, when lenient decisions in very brutal rape cases had merited little public attention? Economist and theorist Ursula Barry assesses the importance of this particular case as being directly attributable to the fact that for the first time ever an Irish rape victim had chosen to give up her anonymity. 'The first thing that struck me about the case, and something that has stayed with me more than anything else since, is the courage of the woman involved. To me it had echoes of the meeting in the Mansion House many years ago when a woman stood up and said she was an unmarried mother and that was the first time that that had happened. Looking back it seems extraordinary how difficult it was in those days for a woman to come out publicly and say that. The broader issue in the Kerwick case is the situation of individual women dealing with the courts and having their response to a situation determined by the legal system. But also there is the fundamental status of women in this society being defined by its institutions.'

Ursula Barry also sees parallels between the Lavinia Kerwick case and the X case (the case which involved a fourteen-year-old rape victim who was prohibited by the High Court and the Attorney General's office from leaving Ireland to have an abortion in Britain. The case was brought as a direct result of the constitutional ban on abortion arising from the 1983 amendment to the Irish constitution and article 40.3.3). 'A question raised as a result of the X case is whether a society feels it was right to circumscribe or limit the rights of individual women. In the Lavinia Kerwick case a woman had attempted to follow all the appropriate paths that she is allowed, a police investigation, the courts, and yet the society is not willing to take responsibility for the outcome of that case.' Ursula Barry's assessment, that in the X case the state is intervening and in the Kerwick case the state is refusing to intervene sums up, she says, the dilemma facing this country at present: 'that two women can be sacrificed or set aside for the greater good of our moral, legal and social institutions'.

What is equally relevant is that very complex issues are being debated by focusing upon the lives of individuals. This is not a new phenomenon. In other countries legal change has been spurred on by the seeming anomalies in a particular case, but it does have its inherent dangers. In the days following the massive publicity given to Lavinia Kerwick, the broad issue of violence against women was diluted into a discussion of the victim's character. For women in particular, trying to find ways in which the victim has been responsible for her own fate, absolves us of the need to take action on her behalf and releases us from the fear that we may be equally at risk.

Academic and EC researcher Pauline Conroy Jackson sees a strong parallel between what is happening in Ireland in relation to women and violence, and the situation elsewhere in Europe. 'Violence against women has recently become an issue in two countries, Ireland and Italy. The reasons are different in that in Italy it's a collapse of all the values, moral, political and philosophical, and a crisis of confidence in the Italian state and a very central issue is the corruption in business. In Italy the women's movement has targeted both violence against women by the Mafia and violence within the family. In Ireland it is a crisis of some values, philosophical, religious and moral; the profit and political systems are more or less intact apart from some scandals. I identify this question of violence against women as being related to the questioning of the values of a society, the value of a human being by her sex and the value of her child; the two go together. In Italy and Ireland the abuse of children is an issue as important as the abuse of women.'

'Therefore,' she says, 'in a country where a low value is assigned to a woman citizen, as soon as the values of that society are questioned, then the position of women is exposed. In both Ireland and Italy women have been assigned an inferior role in society. When those societies are in turmoil, as they are at present, it is women and children who bear the brunt of the resultant violence.'

What makes Ireland different to other countries on the issue of violence against women is that the violence is perpetrated against women in a country where a unique role has been assigned to women in Irish culture. The fact is that the reality of Irish women's lives is often at odds with this role. 'The images assigned women in Irish society,' Ursula Barry says, 'include their strength, their power and their very central role as mothers. That is the most powerful image of Irish women and one that has dominated Irish literature.' What happens though to the woman who steps outside of that image? In particular, Barry sees an analogy between the less muted public reaction to the case of a young Donegal girl who gave evidence in Dublin's Central Criminal Court earlier this year of sexual abuse involving a number of men in her community, and the Kerwick case. A report in *The Sunday Tribune* newspaper, which included an interview with the young girl, carried a description of how the seven men accused in the case were given the kind of welcome usually reserved for a winning football team when they returned home to Donegal. 'How could a community in any way celebrate the protracted sexual abuse of a young girl?' Barry asks. 'One of the things that seemed quite clear is that it was as if the family did not have social status. Once some kind of cycle of abuse starts the victim has no existence. For a strong enough section of the community to cut off from her like that, it was as if she became a non-person. She was tied into some kind of symbol of the fallen girl; fundamentally whatever fault there was, was put at her doorstep. What's happened in the wake of the Kerwick case is that women are saying, you can't do that, we refuse to accept that.'

The issue of violence against women also touches on how we see ourselves as a people. Again, to quote Pauline Conroy Jackson, 'There is a notion of the Irish people, which we have internalised, as being generous, hospitable, easy-going and well-disposed towards others. How do we balance that view and the fact that we could be vindictive, vicious and deeply nasty? The issue of violence against women in all its forms indicates that there are tendencies of this kind not just among one or two individuals but in the culture. We're paying a very high price here for the suppression of these issues since the foundation of the state.'

Nowhere is this suppression more apparent than in the official figures in relation to what have been termed 'sexual crimes'. In 1980, for example, a total of seventeen sexual crimes (all types) were reported to the police. By 1983, the new legislation on rape, the Criminal Law Rape Act 1981, had begun to take effect and 282 cases were reported to the police, rising to 316 by 1985. Of the cases reported in 1985, a little over half ended in prosecution. While the police had a total of 316 cases reported to them in 1985, the Dublin Rape Crisis Centre was dealing with 1,004 cases, rising to 1,372 in 1986. The Department of Health also saw a large increase in reports of child sexual abuse in the 1980s, jumping from thirty-seven confirmed cases in 1983 to 274 in 1986 and reaching 600 by 1990. In relation to wife abuse, the statistics also show a gap between reporting and reality. The first Commission on the Status of Women (1972) for instance addressed itself to a wide-ranging series of recommendations on issues affecting Irish women, but none of its forty-nine recommendations and seventeen suggestions contained any mention of battered women. The first comprehensive study on the plight of women who use women's refuges was carried out in 1986 by Maeve Casey. Of the 127 women surveyed in her report published by Women's Aid, 88 per cent reported that they had been 'battered for years' before they approached a refuge, while 64 per cent reported that they experienced violence on a monthly basis or more frequently. The women's refuge in Rathmines, Dublin, just one of Ireland's six refuges, deals with about ten emergency calls per day.

'In all of these areas, rape, child abuse and battering,' Róisín McDermott of Dublin Women's Aid explains, 'what we're seeing is a breaking of the silence. We have women contacting us in their sixties who wait until then to get out of a long-term violent situation. The problem is, of course, that while the voluntary agencies are developing and changing all the time to meet the increased needs of women, the official agencies and, most especially, the law is locked into a set of piecemeal responses. When they come under pressure they move a little bit, but no-one is examining the underlying causes of violence to see how they can be changed.'

Pauline Conroy Jackson sums up the official response to victims of violence as being the 'Texas home-care' school of reaction, or in other words, 'do-it-yourself'. 'The victim is supposed to go to some kind of self-help group. There's all this talk about victims needing our help and support, but where are they supposed to get it? It is presumed that there will always be well-meaning voluntary groups prepared to do the job without any proper financial backing.'

In Conroy Jackson's opinion the Irish state has in certain instances ceded the protection of citizens to individuals and voluntary groups. 'The state has made a decision not to vindicate the rights of some citizens. An example is the lack of public transport at night on a national basis. That would, at the very least, be a statement that women had the right to go out at night. That doesn't of course address the question that a lot of the violence against women takes place in their own homes; nor does it deal with the fact that teachers in schools are seeing inappropriate behaviour among teenagers, but they haven't the resources to deal with it. If Justice Flood had decided that the young man's behaviour in raping Lavinia Kerwick was a sign of disturbance and that he needed treatment then there wouldn't have been anywhere to send him. If there are no treatment centres then it must be because the state thinks there's no need for them.'

A major problem with the state's reaction to violence within the family and relationships is the tendency to see these as being 'personal problems' for which the state cannot regulate. Historically, Ireland has found itself in a double quandary when formulating family policy. On the one hand the constitution guarantees certain inalienable rights to the family, by which it is meant to regulate itself. The effect of this, as Alan Shatter TD points out in *Family Law in the Republic of Ireland*, is that legal reform in Ireland has come about through pressure as opposed to well-researched and thought-out social policy. And, on the other hand, the catholic church's control over moral development excused successive administrations from debating or legislating on the questions of violence within the family or relationships. The whole area of marital rape for example is an illustration of this point. Giving evidence to the Joint Oireachtas Committee on Women's Rights on behalf of the police in 1986, Chief Superintendent Michael Casey was asked about the possible police reaction to enforcing a law on rape within marriage. 'I was hoping you would not bring me into the bedroom,' the Chief Superintendent replied. When Deputy Madeleine Taylor Quinn pointed out that 'there are many women in the country, particularly in rural areas where they do not have the same resources, facilities or agencies as they have in urban areas, but where this is happening,' Chief Superintendent Casey expanded on his original point. 'It is not so much reluctance as that it is a delicate issue. If I could borrow a phrase from ecclesiastical legislation, when they get married they are no longer two, they are two in one, and they are entitled to the natural love-play that would exist between any husband and wife. There may be an objection on occasions. That is an issue that would be very hard to tease out.'

A senior Irish police officer gave the following overview on the effects which changes in the law, like the provision of barring and protection orders and new legislation on rape have had on the police.

'Before the 1970s women were not really a legal entity in Irish law. Women lived in an essentially stagnant male-oriented society with very limited statutory rights. Traditionally, meddling in a dispute between husband and wife was not encouraged in the police force, if it could at all be prudently avoided. It was regarded as a "grey area" which was best left to the remedies of civil law to sort out. All the police could do was to prosecute the offending husband for assault or breach of the peace. I can recall many cases during my own years of service where the wife failed to turn up in court to give evidence against a husband, persuaded perhaps by her husband's relatives or her own relatives not to shame her children by giving evidence against their brother/father in court. At present when the police are called to a home where there is a family dispute in progress they go there as peace-makers. If they can, they persuade a drunken husband to "'sleep it off". It was disheartening in the past, from the police point of view, to try and deal with cases of domestic violence because our hands were tied. If the case came to court it was on the basis of being a common assault. What woman was going to go through with a case like that and know that she would have to go back and share a home with the man afterwards? In some cases women died because there was no way of taking the man out of the home. It was quite common for us in the 1950s and 1960s to be called out on a Friday and Saturday night and be able to do nothing except give the husband a warning. A lot of the time the violence started after the husband came home drunk, and what was equally frightening was that if you knew the family you'd know that the women had been beaten in that family for generations. The court system was biased against women; there were very few women lawyers, no women Judges or women jury members so that the woman's point of view was never heard.'

The same police officer is particularly pleased, he says, by the new openness in reporting rape cases and he tells the story of an incident in his own career that deeply affected him. 'We were carrying out a murder investigation and discovered in the course of door-to-door enquiries that a number of women had been raped by an individual who was later found guilty of the murder. The moral climate of the time meant of course that none of them had come forward and made a report. If they had the police would have been able to watch the area he operated in. I have no doubt in my mind that the woman who was murdered need not have died.'

In the Working Party on Child Sexual Abuse Report (1986), prepared under the auspices of the Irish Council for Civil Liberties, a large number of experts examined child abuse in Ireland. In the section headed 'Child Abuse as an Irish Problem' they covered the particular Irish dimension to sexual abuse. Although referring specifically to children, the factors which they credited with having a particular influence on child sexual abuse could be equally applied to all violence against women: 'Problems in identifying and dealing with sexual abuse, such as late disclosure, inadequate legal and social responses, lack of resources and professional discomfort, seem to reflect unresolved moral questions in Irish society which appear too threatening or divisive to debate freely and rationally.' Dealing with the legal attitudes to sexual abuse, the working party argued thus: 'Traditionally the law has legitimated the dominant rights of married men over their wives and also over their children, and these archaic rights are being eroded only in piecemeal fashion. Even though law and society disapprove of violence in general, patriarchal assumptions about the right of husbands to exercise control over wives continue to be held by a significant proportion of the population.'

A contentious aspect of the debate on women and violence is the manner in which exponents of the law interpret that law. On the one hand there is the notion, widely held among lawyers, that the independence of the judiciary must be defended at all costs. And on the other hand there is the argument that lawyers reflect the views

47

of the broader society in relation to women, and that the courts can never be some sort of neutral ground. Lawyers themselves exercise a certain double-think when it comes to analysing these issues. Though they have no qualms about privately discussing the beliefs and prejudices of a particular member of the bench, when they feel themselves under threat from outside pressure groups they insist that Judges are as even-handed as Solomon. There is an added problem in all of this: pressure groups and the legal fraternity are often operating from different scripts even though they may appear to have come to the same conclusion. To the general public, for instance, changes in rape legislation seem to hint at more enlightened attitudes towards women. To the majority of lawyers, these same changes were merely a way of clearing up anomalies within the law. Even those lawyers who would term themselves liberal become angry at the unrealistic expectations of the law which they claim are held by other sections of Irish society. As one leading woman lawyer put it succinctly, 'The law is part of society. Society is inherently biased; you cannot expect the law to be different. The courts cannot provide an answer to everything; too many people expect the courts to provide solutions to what are essentially social problems.'

Noreen Byrne, Director of Parents Alone in Coolock and a long-time campaigner on social issues, has a particular interest in what *really happens* in court as opposed to what's *supposed* to happen. 'Our experience in Parents Alone is that we spend as much time explaining to people what the actual legal situation is, teaching them how to retain a sense of their own personal power, and how to get around the law, as we do explaining the law. A lot of the time we're giving people advice even though they have solicitors. They're told, this is black and white, and we on the other hand are teasing out the issues so that they can get the most out of a bad situation.' Noreen Byrne sees lawyers not so much as a class in Irish society, but as 'a caste'. She feels strongly that though the law is a practical expression of the attitudes of Irish society, in trying to reform the law, the basic feminist message, that women have an equal right to walk the streets at night or be safe in their own homes, is lost. In the days following Justice Flood's decision, some women's groups were accused of attempting to extract vengeance from the law, a claim which they strenuously denied. 'Why were we so afraid to say, yes, we do want vengeance?' Noreen Byrne demands. 'Why shouldn't we feel vengeful? It would be great if we could say, yes, we feel vengeful because Irish men need to hear that in order to understand the impact of the threat of violence. We have a tremendous need in the women's movement to be seen as mainstream and respectable. There's a terrible fear among Irish women about expressing anger. That's an effect of the weakness of the women's movement. We're brought up to be the primary carers, to meet everyone else's needs except our own. Yet we're living in a society where we don't even have the right to our own security, or even 50 per cent of the family home. Ideologically women are seen as the carers in this country. In that context we're not allowed to express our own feelings about a situation.'

Dealing daily with women who are living in violent situations, Byrne is critical of the way Irish society responds to those women who do complain about violence within the family. 'The whole basis of medical treatment in relation to women in Ireland has been one of suppressing anger. You go to a doctor and tell him you're upset because your husband is spending his dole money on drink and then comes home and beats you up. And what does the doctor do? He gives you valium. You're the one with the problem.' In the wake of the Lavinia Kerwick case, as Byrne sees it, 'women did not go out and beat up men, they did not go out breaking windows or destroying property yet they were accused of looking for revenge.' A major problem in her estimation is the gap between men's and women's experience when they attempt to discuss violence and its effects. 'When we're talking about violence we're acting out our feelings. For men it's an intellectual issue. If I hear footsteps behind me at night, for instance, I have to make a decision about what to do. I'm on my guard immediately. The person walking behind me could be a very decent person, but I can't depend on that, so I walk out from the kerb towards the road. You could intellectualise about that all you like, but the fact is that our society allows men to be violent to women and doesn't want to stop it. If it did we would have programmes in schools telling boys that violence was not acceptable. Irish women make up half the citizens of this country. Why should we spend our lives living in fear when the other half doesn't live that way. I'm getting older and I'm trying hard to keep the fear at bay, otherwise you just wouldn't survive; but I cannot ignore the fact that Irish society is becoming more violent.'

The overall increase in the level of violence is one that is well documented by the police. What has changed, many of those working in the area agree, is that for women in particular the fear of sexual assault has greatly increased over the last ten years. Prior to that many women would have felt, whether rightly or wrongly, that sexual violence was a problem for younger women only, while older women would worry more about muggings and robbery. For the elderly in particular, the fear of violence during a break-in can be overwhelming, but it is only in the past decade or so that elderly women would have begun to feel themselves at risk from sexual violence. Olive Braiden, Director of the Dublin Rape Crisis Centre, is unsure whether there is an increasing trend towards sexual assaults on elderly women or whether women are now more likely to admit that this has happened to them. What she does say in a general comment on sexual assault is that 'the level of violence is higher, there are more gang-rapes, the degree of violence used in assaults is higher. The level of violence in society has increased and that spills over into attacks on women. We are seeing many many more attacks on elderly women where there's rape with violence.' The vexed question of the links between videos and violence is one that also concerns Olive Braiden. 'The availability of violent videos is now widespread and it appears to be respectable. If parents are allowing these videos to be shown in the home it appears as if they too are accepting them.'

In a research paper on a pilot programme for young sex offenders Kieran McGrath, chairperson of the Irish Association of Social Workers, analysed some of the underlying causes of the young sex offender's behaviour. All of this group had been involved in sexual assaults on young children. Only one of the group of eight, who were aged between thirteen and fifteen, had been sexually abused as a child, but all of the eight had watched violent and pornographic videos. According to Dorothy Morrisey, Director of Limerick Rape Crisis Centre, the counsellors at the centre have noticed an increase both in gang-rapes and the ways in which women are being raped. 'I feel that there's a strong correlation between pornography and sexual violence. Obviously that's not the only reason for the violence but what is worrying us is the increase in the number of young offenders in this area and what it bodes for the future ... .'

Despite the fact that the media has been credited with highlighting both the level of violence against women and inconsistencies in sentencing, it has also been held partly responsible for what has been happening. Bishop Michael Smith, after the Kerwick case, accused the media of being partly responsible for the downward trend in 'moral values'. Bishop Smith claimed that moral values in Ireland were being repeatedly undermined by the media and politicians who see catholic teachings as 'fair game' for attack. The bishop told those taking part in the annual Meath diocesan pilgrimage that many of the social ills that were associated with other developed countries have now become part of Irish life. 'Rape was a major news story because of its rarity. Sadly this is no longer the case. Today even the young are not immune to risk and injury,' he said in a newspaper report. These 'sad changes' in our society have resulted, he added, from the persistent undermining of moral values. 'As a country we are experiencing more and more the sad consequences that arise from a breakdown in moral values ... . Unfortunately the primary sufferers will be women and the young.'

In the aftermath of the Kerwick case, junior justice minister Willie O'Dea congratulated women's groups and the media for having highlighted the issue of violence against women. For those working within the media the treatment afforded violence against women sometimes places them in an invidious position. There is no doubt that media reporting of court cases has been the major spur in bringing public attention to discrepancies in sentencing. On the other hand women often find that in reading 'shock-horror' headline stories of attacks on women and children they literally become prisoners within their own homes. On the morning of a 'Reclaim the Night' women's march in Dublin in August 1992 a woman contacted Maeve Lewis, education officer with the Dublin Rape Crisis Centre, to ask her for details about the march. 'She told me that she would love to come in to it, but she lived in the suburbs and was afraid to make her way home afterwards,' said Maeve.

North American research on newspaper coverage of rape and sexual assaults shows how a disproportionate number of newspaper column inches are given over to assaults on women as a percentage of all assaults. Even though police may give reporters' details of attempted serious assaults which the women managed to avert, these rarely make the headlines. When asked, women themselves expressed a certain dissatisfaction with the kind of information given in media accounts of attacks on women. Most women for instance wanted to know more about the location of the rape, lighting in the area, proximity to public transport, how the victim was overwhelmed, whether that particular area had a high number of assaults, and descriptions of the attacker. In other words women wanted the newspaper reports to enable them to take precautionary measures as opposed to stopping them from stepping outside their own doors.

Reports of court cases involving sexual violence can also be a source of disquiet for women. The problem for journalists is that they can only write about what actually happened in the courtroom. If the evidence given in court involves a detailed analysis of the assault without any balancing testimony on its effect on the victim then that is what will end up in the newspapers. The fact that rape trials can become a form of public pornography has been documented by those who analyse the social aspects of law. Particular trials are often packed out with lawyers, police and members of the public who have nothing whatsoever to do with the case. Within newspapers themselves, the 'copy' which comes up from the court can sometimes be changed, if an editor feels that certain details are not necessarily in the public interest. That depends very much though on the individual editor taking a moral stance which she or he knows editors in rival newspapers may not adopt.

What the media cannot be held responsible for however, is the fact that women are reporting assaults in increasing numbers. Shooting the messenger will not stop that nor would it make it any easier for victims if all reports of violent crime were to disappear from newspapers, radio and television. Many of the women interviewed for this book attributed their recognition that they were not the only victims of violence and that there was somewhere to go to get help, to media coverage of issues such as violence in the home and incest.

4

A woman is not a punchbag

Louise is so tiny that from a distance one is sure she is no more than eleven or twelve years of age. Up close the lines of tiredness on her face put her somewhere in her mid-thirties; in fact she is only twenty-five. Those who know her well have told me that talking to Louise is 'a tonic, she is so good-humoured'. All of this makes the subject we are about to discuss seem even more bizarre.

Louise has suffered near-strangulation, she has been thrown against walls while her head has been continuously bashed off them, and for a long period of time her injuries were so bad that she was ashamed to leave her own home. Living as she did in a small community in the heart of Ireland, she was never aware, she says, that there was anywhere for her to go in order to escape being beaten by her husband. 'I never even knew such places like refuges existed. Maybe if I had, I would have left sooner.'

As it was, Louise was beaten on a regular basis for almost seven years. 'My mother died when I was very young, and my father became ill shortly after I married, so there was no-one I could have gone to, even if I had thought of telling someone.' The only indication she had before she got married that her husband might one day become violent towards her was that he was 'quick-tempered'. She also had a niggling doubt about getting married, but 'he kept insisting that it would be the makings of us.' The first beating came when she was six months pregnant. 'He was out having a few drinks so I was tired and went to bed. He didn't like the fact that I had gone to bed without him. I woke up, with him sitting on top of me and calling me a bitch. All I could think of was to try and calm him down so I wouldn't lose the baby.'

From then on the beatings occurred on a regular basis

and Louise was constantly assessing her husband's moods. 'If he came home with a certain look on his face I knew I was in for it, and nothing I'd do would be right for him. He'd tell me that he wanted his dinner very hot, and I'd heat it up for him, and then he'd say it was too hot and throw it on the floor. One night he'd come in and say he was going out and didn't want dinner. Five minutes later he'd come into the kitchen and say, "Where's my dinner?" '

On some occasions the violence was so bad that Louise would leave her house at three or four o'clock in the morning and walk the roads around her home, hoping that her husband would have calmed down or fallen asleep by the time she got back. A neighbour who told Louise that she knew what was going on, persuaded her not to go back home after one particularly vicious beating. The neighbour phoned the police who accompanied Louise back to her home. They asked her husband to come with them, but rather than taking him to a police station they merely drove him into the village and left him there. An hour later he was back home again. 'I went through one month when the beatings were so bad,' Louise says, 'that I never left the house, not even to walk my daughter to school. Eventually one of the children's teachers got worried and called up to see me, but I didn't go to the door – my husband did – my face was so bad.' If she was ever asked about an injury Louise told neighbours that she had fallen or bumped into something. She never went to hospital until the night when her husband kicked her full-force in the back. 'I was in a lot of pain and I went up to the bathroom and started to pass blood. A neighbour took me to the hospital and the nurse asked me what had happened. I told her that I had fallen and she said, "A fall couldn't have caused that; that's more like a kick. Don't worry," she said. "You're not the first I've seen like that." I think that that was when I began to realise that other women were going through the same thing as me.' The kick damaged Louise's kidneys and has caused her long-term pain.

After the birth of her third child, Louise had a hysterectomy. 'After that he would kick me in the stomach and say that I was no good for anything. I couldn't even have children.' Other injuries she suffered included burns. 'He would ask for coffee and say it wasn't hot enough, and then he'd throw it at me.' Although he drank alcohol, Louise says that her husband beat her whether he was drunk or sober. 'It got to the stage where I was saving a little bit from my house-money so that when he'd run out of money, I'd be able to give him two pounds. That way I'd be saved from another beating. Sometimes even that didn't work. He'd get annoyed that I had kept money back from him and he'd give me a beating for that. If he came in and I was in bed, he'd call me down just to light his cigarette.'

The obvious question, why didn't Louise leave, is answered quite pragmatically by her. 'Where could I go with three children? When I heard there was a refuge I went there.' The night she left, Louise says, she had run out of choices. 'He was going to kill me whether I stayed or I went. He used to say that if I went to the police, he might go to jail, but he'd come back and finish me off. That last night, he came in and kicked me and punched me and banged my head off the wall. Then he told me to go up to bed, and when he came into the bedroom he told me to take all my clothes off. Then he said, "Go and stand in the corner," and he started to make remarks about how thin I was. Then he began to spit at me, until I was covered in spit. That was worse than all the beatings, just lying there in the corner, waiting for him to go to sleep. I crawled across the floor and got my clothes and then I went in for one last look at the children. I knew I wouldn't be able to take them with me until I got some place for them.'

After spending a year in a refuge, Louise was re-housed and got her children back. She then applied for a barring order so that her husband would not come to her new home. 'What I didn't know was that the barring order would have my address on it, so he found me. He still had access to the children, but I was bringing them to him in a neighbour's house. When he found out where I lived he arrived one morning and broke in the back door. I was in the front room and he jumped on me and pushed me to the ground, and started banging my head off the floor. I started to black out. A neighbour who had called in tried to get him off me but she couldn't, so she screamed at her daughter to run and call the police. She told him that the police were on their way and he got off me and ran.'

Having been arrested for that attack Louise's husband was later released on bail. Louise feels quite helpless in the face of these random assaults. 'There is a policeman who has been dealing with the case, but if I ring the station and he's not there, no-one else can tell me what's going on, whether they're looking for my husband, or they've caught him.' Although still worried about what her husband might do to her, Louise's life is better in every other way, she says. 'The kids are great now. They used to be coming out in their night-clothes trying to stop him from beating me. Now they're much happier. I have a whole new life. Before I could never have spoken to my neighbours; now I talk to the woman next door. I can manage my money, put money aside and buy a can of paint and do up my house. I would say to anyone else in the same position, you don't have to stay. A woman is not a punchbag. You don't have to put up with that.'

For Róisín McDermott of Women's Aid in Dublin, life-histories like Louise's are a tangible expression of a number of developments in Irish society. The most pertinent is the increase in the numbers of women trying to leave violent homes. 'While no refuge will turn women away, there is a desperate shortage of accommodation,' Róisín McDermott explains. 'In the first six months of this year, the Eastern Health Board spent £54,000 on emergency bed and breakfast accommodation, yet the big issue for Women's Aid has been trying to prove the need for more refuges. The Health Board says there is an adequate supply of accommodation, but at the refuge in Rathmines in 1991, 357 families had to be referred elsewhere because the Rathmines refuge could not accommodate them. Although a woman may go to her nearest refuge for help, the shortage of accommodation means that she may be referred on to another refuge. In some cases women are so afraid that they go to the refuge furthest away from their own home.'

The women arriving at the refuge are offered different types of support. 'Firstly, for a woman who believes that her husband is capable of change and who wants to go back, counselling is available. Then there are women who are going through the whole legal system, protection orders, barring orders, custody. Thirdly, there is a group of women who come into the refuge, take out all the various orders and then go for a full separation and rehousing.'

As well as having a consultative role in the work of Dublin's Rathmines Refuge, Women's Aid also runs a telephone help line, on a voluntary basis. 'We are seeing an increasing problem,' Róisín McDermott says, 'where the abuser is becoming more clever. He will for instance have punched the woman in the stomach, the kidneys, generally in areas where he knows he won't mark her, and in middle-class families in particular, he will never mark her face. Middle-class women don't tend to come to refuges. The social need to hide the fact that they have been abused is greater for them. Recently a woman who worked in a private nursing home complained to me about the fact that, as she put it, "places like ours are being seen as some kind of refuge; they're sent in here with their pretty smiling faces and then you find that their bodies are covered in bruises." '

Another area of concern for Women's Aid is the increase in verbal and psychological abuse. 'The abuser may have locked the woman in her bedroom every night, he may have starved her, repeatedly raped her, but there's no physical evidence that you can bring to court. The problem with verbal abuse, constantly telling a woman that she's useless, that she's a whore, a prostitute, is that the woman's self-esteem hits rock-bottom. She's in a situation where she's been married for a number of years, she's economically dependent, and the abuser is probably charming to the rest of the world. Because he has one person he can abuse all the time, he can afford to be charming. His partner on the other hand is afraid that no-one will believe her. You also get women who have been abused for years who have never gone near the police. But they would have been admitted to outpatient's departments in hospital with various fractures and broken bones and teeth and even with a number of miscarriages. There's a strong need for medical personnel to be able to identify and record these assaults.'

Along with the actual increase in women coming to organisations like Women's Aid, 'Women have also been disclosing their experience of violent sexual assaults by their partners,' Róisín McDermott says. 'We're coming across the kind of assaults that are usually seen in pornography; women being made to watch blue movies, being tied up, urinated upon, defecated upon. These women are absolutely devastated by what's happened to them, shattered, ashamed, humiliated; they feel so degraded. We have dealt for years with abuse and assault, but in the last few years we're coming across more examples of violent sexual abuse. We had one woman of fifty years, for example, contacting a refuge. She had started experiencing violent sexual abuse, including rape. What we don't know is whether people are lifting the lid and more women are now talking about abuse, or whether the objectification and humiliation of women through pornographic magazines and films has caused abusive men to learn new ways of abusing women.'

The question on the minds of many people reading about wife abuse is to wonder what actually triggers abuse, and why men who appear gentle and charming to the outside world can terrorise their own families over a long period of time. International research in this area suggests that there is no easy analysis of why abuse occurs.

What can be said is that there are a number of factors which are common to most cases of woman-battering. These have been summed up in the British Goverment's *Domestic Violence: Home Office Report 107* as including 'possessiveness and jealousy, demands concerning labour, and money'.

Reviewing the various research studies carried out in this area, the author of the Home Office report was surprised to find that not all episodes of violence occurred as a result of an argument, and where an argument did occur, in over half the cases it had lasted only five or six minutes before the woman was beaten. An enduring stereotype for most people is that battered women nag their husbands until they beat them, and that in some cases there are 'lazy' housewives who irritate their partners into assaulting them. Many battered women, however, use complete compliance with their partner's wishes as a coping strategy when dealing with violence. They will, as in Louise's case, ensure that their husband's dinner is exactly as he orders it to be, regardless of the inconvenience to themselves. Another myth often used to excuse society's inaction in the face of domestic violence is that the victim 'wants to be hit' and stays in a violent relationship because she enjoys it. Looking at this assumption, Home Office Report 107 found that all the available evidence disproved this theory. Citing the most recent research, the report found that out of fifty-nine victims of violence who finished an abusive relationship, only three entered into another violent relationship. What is more relevant to a woman's escape from a cycle of abuse and violence, the bulk of research has shown, is that she has to have some kind of support to help her leave.

'Jean', who until recently was employed as a counsellor to women who have been battered, cites a number of factors which inhibit women from leaving an abusive partner. (In order to preserve the anonymity of those she has counselled 'Jean' did not wish to use her own name.) 'The first and most important thing which keeps women in these violent situations is fear, fear of the violence, fear of what will happen to her after she reports it to someone outside the family. Another vital consideration is the economic issue. When a woman has children to consider she is also very reluctant to put the children's welfare at risk. With a wait of a minimum of six months at the legal aid centres a battered woman has no access to a solicitor. That's just the wait to make an appointment, not including the length of time it will take to go through the courts. If she leaves the family home she may have difficulty in getting back in again, and of course the obvious question is, where is she supposed to go when she leaves? She will usually have to take the children out of school, disrupting their studies. Even if she does go to court, there is no guarantee that the evidence she has, especially if she has not reported to the police, will get her a barring or protection order. Some women say that living with a barring order is actually worse because you never know when he'll break in and attack you; the uncertainty really wears you down. In many cases a woman will have disclosed the abuse to somebody, a member of her family, or a priest, and their attitude may lead her to believe that her first duty is to keep the family intact, no matter what the personal cost. The abuser may tell her that he is going to change if he thinks she's leaving and that will give her some kind of hope. After many years of abuse, her energy is so low that she begins to believe what the abuser is telling her, that she's no use and that she couldn't survive without him.'

For many women, therefore, the decision to leave often comes when they reach a certain point. Marian, a middle-class woman who endured years of abuse says, 'It gets to a point where you think that death would be easier than living like this. I had a bottle of pills. I was ready to take them when I telephoned a refuge. It had got to the stage where I dreaded the evenings when the key would turn in the door and he'd come home.' Marian's husband's obsession with money ruled both their lives, she says. 'It began on our honeymoon. We were both working but he had taken over the money when we were saving to get married. On the honeymoon he wouldn't allow me to buy any presents to bring home, so I'd save a little bit from our daily allowance and buy something small out of it. I didn't complain because he had a way of making me think that what he was doing was for my own good.' When the children came along, she lost whatever little control she had over the family's joint finances. 'He would come home in the evening and check the tank to make sure I hadn't put on the heating during the day. Myself and the kids never ate meat, but he would have to have meat put in front of him every evening. I used to borrow money from my mother to makes ends meet and one day she said she was sick of paying for her grandchildren to eat sausages while he ate meat. So that evening I cooked a cheaper cut of meat for the whole family. He threw the meal at the wall when he saw it.'

Outwardly living a normal lifestyle, married to a busy professional man in a large country town, Marian's days were spent keeping within the strict budget her husband set. 'We had a telephone, but I had to write down every call I made and the length of time. Some days he'd take a connection for the phone with him so that I couldn't use it while he was out.' In the ten years of their marriage, Marian's allowance was never increased, no matter what emergency occurred or what extras her children needed. Her fear of her husband was so great that she lost a great deal of weight. Before approaching her husband with requests for money for the children Marian usually had a vomiting fit from stress. She eventually decided to tell him that she thought they should both go to a marriage guidance counsellor, but she vomited for days before she could ask him. During a marriage guidance session the counsellor asked Marian's husband to show consideration for her as a person by doing something special for her. 'At the next session he was asked what he had done, and he described how he'd been out in the golf-club with a few of his friends at a do and on the way home he'd stopped and bought five Lotto scratch cards, and he'd given me one. The counsellor just put his head in his hands.'

An important factor in Marian's case was her feeling of isolation from both her neighbours and friends. 'I never went out, and I couldn't have friends in the house while he was there. The only social outing I had was to a keep-fit class, but that stopped because he said it cost too much; it was £2.75 per week.' The main violence in Marian's case was mental. Although her husband did throw items at her, she had no physical injuries. The verbal abuse and the feeling of not being loved or cared for devastated her and left her completely lacking in self-confidence. When she left her home and took the children to a refuge, she also set about getting custody. 'At the hearing the Judge said that the family home was preferable to a refuge, for children, so I lost them.' Even now, years later, she still finds it hard to talk about the period she spent without her children. 'I broke down completely in the courtroom. As it turned out, after a year I got them back, but the whole experience was awful.' Asked whether she has ever regretted leaving her marriage and giving up her home, Marian is adamant that she made the best decision. 'I've no regrets. I'd do it all over again. I'm a different person now. Nobody could do those things to me now. You do feel lonely in that you miss having a special relationship with somebody, but I love my life now. I love the quality of my life, not having to hear that key turning in the door and dreading it. I do things that I never realised were normal and that are taken for granted by other people, like going out for a drive with the children on a Sunday.'

The most in-depth report on domestic violence in Ireland *Breaking the Silence: violence in the home* was published in April 1992 by the Policy Research Centre of the National College of Industrial Relations. Commissioned by the Adapt Refuge in Limerick and the Mid-Western Health Board, the two-part report studied the needs and characteristics of the women using the

Adapt Refuge and the circumstances in which they experienced violence. The most frequent triggers (not causes) of attacks on women, the report concluded,

> included alcohol abuse, arguments, jealousy and possessiveness and wanting to exert control over the woman. Almost always the circumstances which trigger the violence are of a trivial nature.

Another of the findings in the Adapt report is that 11 per cent of the women they interviewed had been subjected to sexual assault or rape.

Like some of the women interviewed for the Adapt report, Claire has experienced sexual assault by her husband. For the first two years after she left her home, Claire was afraid to leave the safety of the refuge she had moved to. Soft-spoken and gentle in manner she still has 'The fear' as she calls it. The most dramatic change in her character, she says, is that she talks now. 'I didn't talk for years. People who knew me then probably thought I couldn't talk at all. But by not talking I felt I was avoiding trouble. If I ever went out, it was with my husband, and if people came to talk to me, I never replied to them, so they used to just give up. I knew that if I did say anything he'd be quizzing me afterwards and he'd get annoyed.'

Shortly before she got married, Claire realised that her husband was violent, but by then it was too late. 'I was so afraid of him even then, that I felt I had to marry him.' In the ten years of her marriage Claire was subjected to mental, physical and sexual abuse, and her fear of her husband became all-encompassing. 'Some nights I left the house in my bare feet, and walked around like that, I was so afraid.' She never called the police because she felt the consequences would be worse for her afterwards. Her husband was also careful to mark her body only, not her face. 'I remember one day he hit me, kicked me on the ground, but never in the face.' As she describes these incidents, Claire's whole body hunches over, and her voice becomes barely audible. 'At night he would never let me leave the bedroom. I couldn't open the door in case he was woken up by the light outside. I used to want to go to the toilet but I was afraid that I'd wake him, so I'd lie there with pains in my stomach. So what I used to do after a while was get up and go to the toilet in a jumper. Then every morning I'd wash the jumper out.' The night she left her home, Claire had been beaten all day. Using the excuse that she was supposed to meet a neighbour to go to the supermarket, she managed to get out of the house. 'I just walked around the supermarket for about an hour, buying nothing, just looking at everything. My head was in a spin. I'd gone to a refuge for just a night once before, but when I got home he was much worse; he knew then that I had somewhere to go. But that night I knew he was so angry that he was going to kill me. Afterwards he said to me, "You're lucky you didn't come home. I was waiting for you." ' Now living apart from her husband, Claire admits that she is still afraid of him. 'He said one thing to me, "You won't always be in a refuge," and I've never forgotten those words.'

Asked if they can explain the reasons behind their husbands', behaviour, Louise, Marian and Claire give different answers. 'It's very hard to trust anyone when you come out of a violent situation,' Marian says. 'You wonder is there something wrong with you that you ended up with this kind of person. Then you meet other women and realise that they're all asking the same thing. My husband came from a good family. He had everything he wanted when he was growing up, yet he felt that he could treat me like that. It's a man's world and he felt that as a man he was entitled to make all the decisions. He never really talked to me. I was stupid as far as he was concerned. All he could do was put me down. In a way I feel sorry for him. I believe that he did love me but I can see him now with the children, still not realising how much they need from him. I've tried to ensure that he has a good relationship with them but sometimes I wonder if money is the only thing that's important to him.'

Louise sees her husband's behaviour as being a

reflection of his upbringing. 'His father was violent. He used to say when he beat me, "My father was right, that's all ye women are good for." Sometimes afterwards I'd ask him why he had done it, and he would be surprised. It was as if one part of him just switched off.'

As far as Claire is concerned, her husband has definite mental problems. 'You wouldn't do to a dog the things he did to me. I said that to him once after I left and he was surprised. It was like he never imagined I had feelings.'

For those who deal with the victims of domestic violence, there is very little time and very few resources available to analyse its underlying causes. 'In Women's Aid, we are dealing with the crisis of the victim, and we are dealing with that crisis on a shoe-string,' Róisín McDermott explains. 'We really have had no opportunity to work on the wider issue and see why this is happening. From our experience in the area, we would see this violence as being a combination of the personal history of the abuser and the social, political and economic situation. In my opinion the men who abuse women are often very insecure and they have bought hook, line and sinker the view that men should have power and control over women. I don't believe, however, that you can always use the rationale that men who are abused go on to do the same thing. You cannot condemn boys who've been abused into repeating the pattern. What is interesting is that the programmes which have been most successful with men who batter are the ones which combine mandatory sentencing with mandatory therapy and which confront violent men about their attitudes to women.'

For women who try to leave, the high level of support they require and the low level that is actually available may force many to return to the violent home. Based on her experience as a former counsellor in a refuge, Jean sees the need to keep the family intact as being very important to the women she has counselled. 'There are strong social and family pressures on women in this country to stay in the home and keep the family together. The way we have culturally and religiously defined the family is that it is the cornerstone of our society; so women have great difficulty in disclosing to an outsider that there is something wrong within the family. In lower-income families the big difficulty is that economically women can't leave. In higher-income families there is a higher degree of secrecy and silence, and as with sexual abuse, social workers are more actively involved with lower-income families. The other agencies which women approach, hospitals, priests, the police, may not be able to recognise the signs of abuse. They may not have any training in dealing with women who find themselves in this situation. Although a woman may appear to have more money in a higher-income family, you may find out that she has no access to cash, that all of her spending is controlled and defined by her husband.'

The issue of 'ownership of the woman' in a relationship is one that Jean has also come to identify with abuse. 'When a husband visits a refuge for the first time after his wife has left he is usually extremely angry. He often says things like "she's my wife and I want her out of here". They have so little respect for their wives' ability to think independently that they are sure you have put the idea to leave home into their wives' heads.'

Jean's work has had its own psychological toll on her. 'It has definitely saddened me as a person; it has saddened me to have to face the extent and reality of abuse and to see how the lives of women and children are shattered. There were days when I thought that I couldn't look at the body of another human being covered in bruises. It's impossible to accept the battering that goes on when women are pregnant. Or you come across a woman who's been raped, who still has stitches from having delivered her baby only days before. I said recently to a consultant that when you say things like this to people it's so horrific that they can't imagine it, and he replied, "And it's so common as well". That really shocked me, that he was so accepting of the fact that women would be beaten while they are pregnant. The women are so preoccupied with the pregnancy that their partners feel they themselves are being neglected. There's also the whole area of sexual assault, the use of implements, pornography. I am not alone in having come across the extent of sexual assault against women in the home. What I wonder about is why there is such a deafening silence. Where is the outcry? Where are the human rights agencies? Where are the government enquiries? What has happened to us as women that we've learned to live with this level of assault? Why are we afraid to lift the lid?

Family violence, the official response

In the twelve month period between 1 November 1989 and 31 October 1990, Dublin police had to respond to a total of 3,500 cases of domestic violence. In a report in *The Irish Independent*, security correspondent Tom Brady wrote that 'a vast number of violent attacks on women in the home are not being reported to police because of fears that they could become victims again.' Announcing that a conference on safety for women was being organised by the Department of Justice, Minister Pádraig Flynn was quoted by Brady as saying that 'he believed that assaults in the home should be treated as crimes and dealt with fully by the law. International studies indicated that the level of under-reporting on incidents in the home was as high as 70 per cent, and from the evidence available here, Mr Flynn said that he felt a similar figure existed in this country.' The same report revealed that police are now to receive training in dealing with domestic violence as part of their two-year induction programme at Templemore and will be told how to advise victims and put them in contact with support groups.

The news that the police were willing to become more informed on the issues around domestic violence had been an open secret among the various support groups dealing with victims of violence for some months. None of these groups was prepared to talk publicly about this development, however, in case it would prejudice their relationship with the police. 'In general the police in this country have been the first official group to recognise that there is a problem and they have also been the one group to understand the problems that victims are facing,' one support group spokesperson told me. 'Of course you get the odd ignorant individual police officer on the ground with whom women have problems, but they tend to be the exception rather than the rule. What the police will say to you is that their hands are tied because the courts may not always take the side of the victim.' Where victims of domestic violence have tended to differ with police handling of their situation is on the issue of what they wanted them to do when they were called to the home. Many women want the police to act in their role as arresting officers whereas the individual police officer may decide that the best response is to be a peacemaker. In the Adapt report, for instance, though the majority of women interviewed were happy with their contact with the police, a minority felt that the police had not wanted to get involved in family rows. For women who are not married to their partners there is the added difficulty that they are not entitled to barring or protection orders. The main legal difficulty faced by the police is that domestic violence is so often seen as a private civil matter as opposed to a public criminal matter.

Up to 1976 the only legal remedy available for a wife who was being assaulted by her husband was to take out a summons against her husband for assault. The provision of barring and protection orders has meant that these are now the preferred remedies for women who are being battered. Support groups like Women's Aid complain that the main difficulty with barring orders is that enforcement is erratic and often depends on the attitude of the particular police officers involved. The police say that they have to deal with the frustration of taking someone to court for breach of a barring order and finding that the chances of the defendant receiving serious punishment are minimal. Taking out a barring and protection order usually means applying for a solicitor and, as already mentioned, the long delay in the free legal aid system means that women are being forced to remain in violent situations. Technically, a woman can apply for a barring order by applying directly to a court clerk, but many women are intimidated by the idea that they would in effect be representing themselves in court. Because husbands usually have control of the family finances, they will nearly always engage a solicitor in order to defend themselves against a barring order. In their submission to the Second Commission on the Status of Women, Women's Aid recommended that 'assault on a woman in her home be treated as common assault and that, as such, criminal charges be pressed by the police immediately, thus removing the responsibility for pressing charges from the victim who is in a relationship with the offender'. One of the reasons often given for police reluctance to arrest violent partners is that the victim will later change her mind and refuse to press charges. Dealing with this issue the Adapt report found that of the 129 women in their study who applied for barring orders only 2 per cent later dropped their application. The Adapt study bears out international findings in this area which show that women who are assaulted in the home *do* follow through with charges.

Ruth Torode, lecturer in Sociology in Trinity College Dublin, has administered and taught on a number of training programmes for police, probation officers, childcare and social workers. Dealing with the area of the official attitude to wife abuse she quotes various studies which see the police response as being crucial. 'In Canada for instance there was a policy decision to shift the police role from being one of peace-keeping to law enforcement. They had found that because no consequence followed upon a police call, there was no impact on the level of violence. Then in London Ontario in 1982 they issued an instruction that in their region all domestic violence calls would be treated as a law-enforcement issue. While the number of convictions went up, the number of repeat calls dropped dramatically. While this was perceived as being a success, it was not adopted as a wide-ranging policy. What you have to be careful of is that you don't just issue an instruction to the police without following it up with training and discussion.' According to Torode, there has also been evidence to show that if the police are sympathetic and tell women about refuges, women feel they have some measure of support in changing a violent situation. The official view on barring and protection orders seems to be that they have effectively replaced the need for other support mechanisms for battered women. The Adapt report reveals that when the Limerick refuge, Adapt House, approached the then Minister for Health, Dr Michael Woods, for funding, he queried the need for a refuge in view of the legislation on barring orders.

In the Irish context, domestic violence is being taken more seriously by the police. 'The question is how seriously is it being taken by the other agencies with whom women come in contact?' Torode asks. On this very question the Adapt report found that an equal number of women had approached social workers as had approached the police. 'For the most part,' the report states, 'the women interviewed perceived that the help obtained through social workers had not affected the relationship with their husbands in any significantly positive way.' Other agencies the women contacted included GPs, hospital doctors, marriage counsellors, psychiatrists, psychologists, solicitors and court clerks. The major difficulty for women approaching hospitals is that fear of further beatings may prevent them from actively seeking help or may cause them to lie about their injuries. Some refuges are now in negotiation with local hospitals as a preparation for having an input into emergency and accident procedure. As these negotiations are at an early stage none of the parties involved were willing to talk about them on the record. What they will say, however, is that the average large hospital may see one battered woman a day in the outpatients section. Most of the medical personnel know that these women are being attacked, but they are unsure as to how they should get involved. In contrast with their experience with official agencies, the majority of the women in the Adapt report felt that going to a refuge had been a positive experience. A feeling noted by many of these women was that they had been 'released from fear', that at last they had some peace.

An anomaly in the way we officially treat violence in the home, as Ruth Torode sees it, is that though mechanisms are in place to remove children from abusive situations, there are no such facilities for women, 'nor do we seem to attach importance to the long-term effects on children of their mothers being beaten.' After they leave the refuge situation women deal with often overwhelming feelings of isolation and loneliness. A report, *Silent No More*, currently being carried out for the Combat Poverty Agency by Second Chance, a self-help group for women who have left abusive relationships, lists a number of the problems women in this situation have. These include 'the loneliness of life on one's own, on-going emotional distress, the continuation of the threat and the experience of abuse by one's former partner and the lack of a back-up support system to provide support in dealing with on-going advice and information needs. The lack of understanding of the level of violence and its effects on women were mentioned both by the women interviewed in the Second Chance and the Adapt reports. The Second Chance report calls for:

> the promotion of a public education drive and the integration of specific modules on violence against women into the training of relevant professionals such as police, medical staff and social workers, and the funding of an extensive research project to establish a realistic estimate of the extent of the incidence of violence against women in the home in Ireland.

The Adapt report found that for the women they interviewed the first attack they had suffered was completely unexpected. The very unexpectedness of the violence is seen by women as leaving them powerless either to try to prevent or stop the attack. Women's initial response to the violence includes shock and fear, and they very often blame themselves for the attack. Some (of the abusers), while expressing regret, suggest that the woman herself was to blame, thereby adding to her confusion and distress. A significant issue raised in the report is the need to develop a general awareness of the nature of violence and of the fact that once it happens it is likely to recur and that its frequency and severity increases over time. Women stress the importance of 'breaking the silence' about the violence and of seeking help at an early stage.

5

The hidden prisoners

When the Limerick Rape Crisis Centre first came into existence, over twelve years ago, it did not have a premises from which it could operate. The individual women who had started the centre answered enquiries from phones in their own homes. Counselling was carried out in cars, hotel lobbies and coffee-shops. Even now, years on from those humble beginnings, the Rape Crisis Centre in Limerick shares a building with a number of other companies. 'If it was like Dublin, and this was our building, with only one front door, I don't think we'd get anyone coming to see us,' the centre's administrator, Dorothy Morrisey says. Though a large community, with a population of over 80,000, the feeling locally is that everybody knows everybody else in Limerick. For the women who come to the centre therefore it is important that it shares a premises with other concerns; anybody seen going in could be going to a number of different offices. The issue of confidentiality is an important one for each of the rape crisis centres in Ireland, but it is particularly important in smaller communities. The plus side of being part of the community is that local rape crisis centres benefit from a greater degree of co-operation with other agencies working in the same general area. Some Judges outside Dublin for instance have been willing to read research information supplied by outside agencies. Again, this is such a potentially controversial area that no-one will speak on record about it. The feeling seems to be that there are Judges who wish to become 'better-informed,' especially when dealing with complex questions like the protection of children in child sexual abuse cases, but the word 'training' is absolutely taboo.

The fact that rape crisis centres have become so well-integrated into the communities in which they operate does not however mean that they are not constantly short of funds. The Limerick Rape Crisis Centre, for instance, in its twelve year's existence, has only received official funding twice; on both occasions these were once-off grants of £10,000 and £5,000 respectively. The only other public funds it has access to is a £2,000-a-year grant from the Mid-Western Health Board. This year, for the first time, along with all of the regional rape crisis centres the Limerick Centre is to get base-line support of £25,000 a year from the Department of Health. If nothing else this is a measure of increased public awareness of the valuable work that rape crisis centres are doing. The Limerick Centre sees an average of between nine and fourteen clients per day. Like the country's other rape crisis centres the staff are seeing their client numbers increase each year, but do not know whether there has been an increase in reporting or in the actual incidence of assaults on women. What they can confirm, however, is that the type of assaults have become more vicious, with more gang-rapes, use of implements and forced oral sex.

'Young women have usually been the main targets of assaults,' Dorothy Morrisey says, 'even though it is a myth that only young women are raped. Older women are probably less likely to come and get counselling. We have also noticed an increase in the number of women coming in and disclosing marital rape. For so long women didn't see themselves as being raped when forced sex happened within marriage. It seems to go hand-in-hand with wife-battering. Up to the time of the new rape legislation, marital rape was not criminalised. Now a woman would know that she can bring charges, but obviously she's going to need the same medical evidence as in all rape cases.'

Not all of the rape victims who contact a rape crisis centre are reporting a rape that has recently occurred. People attend who have been raped in the past but who have suppressed what has happened and perhaps never told anybody about it. 'Very often where the rape or abuse has happened in the past, it surfaces again,' Dorothy

Morrisey explains. In rural areas, or even in small towns, it is very difficult for women to 'bring attention' to what has happened to them, by reporting a sexual assault or rape to the police. 'Less than 10 per cent of our clients make reports to the police. The perception still is that what they will have to go through in a court-case will be horrific. If somebody comes in we give them non-directive counselling. Obviously we're delighted if they decide to go through with a court-case, but at the same time we're not saying to the person, "Yes, you have to do this." ' Those working in rape crisis centres are becoming increasingly frustrated with the legal system and its treatment of rape victims.

Dorothy Morrisey agrees that she has begun to wonder about the efficacy of going to court. 'What is actually in it for the rape victim? Nothing, except that she is doing her social duty,' she says. In order to help people understand what happens when a woman makes a formal complaint of rape to the police, she describes the whole procedure step-by-step. 'Firstly if the victim contacts us, we will go with her to the police-station. She is entitled to have a policewoman present. No matter where she is, or how small the village is, she can wait for a policewoman to come from the nearest station. The first thing that happens is the taking of forensic evidence. You can ask for your own GP but you do need a doctor who is familiar with court procedure and taking evidence. The policewoman has to be present for the taking of forensic evidence. There is a kit available which goes into an enormous amount of detail. This whole procedure takes about two to three hours. Then you go back to the station to make a statement and that can take any length of time. It would not be unknown for us to drive somewhere to meet a victim in the afternoon and still be going through these procedures into the early hours of the following morning. The statement taken is very lengthy and every single detail has to be documented. All of that evidence then goes to the Director of Public Prosecution's (DPP) office and there's a long, long wait in order to discover whether there's sufficient evidence for a prosecution or not. If the case does go to court, the victim is simply a witness. When the defendant gets a suspended sentence nobody understands how horrific that is for the woman involved, knowing that *he's* still out there.'

What makes Dorothy Morrisey particularly angry is that 'the police do such terrific work, and the law lets them down. I remember one police officer saying to me that any case that goes to court is a genuine case.' The role played by the prosecuting counsel is one that is often hard for the victim to understand. 'The prosecuting counsel never meets with the victim until about four or five minutes before the case is due to begin,' Dorothy Morrisey elaborates. 'They never give the victim information while the book of evidence is being put together, they never tell her whether the defendant is going to plead guilty or not, or when the case is due to come up, or what is actually in the book of evidence. When the victim is in court, she is literally on her own. There is no-one protecting her from all kinds of degrading cross-examination. She doesn't know who's supposed to be on her side. The defence have much more to fight for. The defence counsel is paid for every day she or he spends in court; the prosecuting counsel is paid a set rate. There's no feeling of the prosecuting counsel fighting the case.'

For 'Eileen', a twenty-three-year-old from a small village in the West of Ireland, the points made by Dorothy Morrisey are depressingly familiar. When she was raped by a former boyfriend, the case went to trial but while he was convicted of assault, he was found not guilty of rape. Eileen's story begins when she met her boyfriend 'Tom' at the age of nineteen. 'When we were first going out together everything was grand, but when we both moved to a town a long distance away from my family, he started becoming very possessive.' After some months, Tom's treatment of Eileen became increasingly more violent, and she moved to another town to get away from him. He followed her there and told her that he was willing to change. 'I don't know how he got my address, but I began to feel as though I'd never get away from him. I moved twice, to two other places and each time he followed me and created a lot of trouble. I even went to London at one stage and he still tracked me down.' After her last encounter with Tom, Eileen left the new town that she was in and came home to her parents. 'I was so afraid of him I literally left in the middle of the night without a jacket.'

After an interval of several weeks Tom arrived at Eileen's parent's house. 'I knew he was going to do that. I hadn't been able to relax for the whole three weeks.' When he asked her to come for a walk to talk about their relationship, Eileen agreed to do so, sure that he wouldn't attempt to assault her when her family was so close at hand. 'He walked me down to a nearby river and that was where he raped me. The whole time all I could keep thinking of was that he would try to kill me.' Some people walking nearby heard Eileen's screams and called the local policeman. When he arrived, Tom assured him that everything was all right, but the policeman became uneasy when he saw that Eileen had blood and bruising on her face. He asked Eileen to come down to the nearby station and there she told him what had happened. 'They arrested Tom for questioning and I was taken to see a doctor. She was very nice, but the whole examination was terrible; it was nearly like being raped again. It took an awful long time, and then they took me back to the station and I was brought out to where it had happened, and then back to the station again.'

Eileen had been assaulted at around seven o'clock in the evening, but it was five o'clock in the morning before she got home. 'Then I got up after about three hours and went back down to the station to make another statement. The file was sent to the DPP and it came up much quicker than anyone had expected. It was about five months afterwards that the trial was held.' Eileen was, she says, 'still in a state of shock even though it was a few months later. I was so bad that I had to go to the doctor and he put me on anti-depressants. The week before the case, I didn't eat or sleep. When I got to the court it was much worse than I had expected it to be. The police told me that it was going to be bad, giving evidence, but it was much much worse. I don't blame other women for not going through with cases. It was worse than being raped.'

The courtroom was packed with men, Eileen says, not all of them people involved with the case. The fact that the evidence alleged that Tom had forced Eileen into certain sexual acts had attracted a number of 'sightseers'. On the witness-stand Eileen was subjected to a very strenuous cross-examination by the defence counsel. 'He tried to make out that because Tom had been my boyfriend he couldn't have *forced* sex on me. He asked me the same question in ten different ways.' At one stage, while trying to describe what had happened to her, Eileen broke down in the witness box. 'His barrister said that I was fooling no-one, trying to look for sympathy from the jury. What he kept saying was that Tom and I had had lots of rows when we were going out together and that what had happened was nothing new.'

The defence case hinged around this notion of a 'volatile' relationship and accusations that Eileen herself liked rough and unusual sexual practices. 'They were coming out with things that were just unbelievable. The whole point of it seemed to be to run me down. There was photographic evidence of my injuries but the jury was not allowed to see it due to a technicality. Then they had a doctor who had never examined me but who had read the reports and who said that my injuries should have been worse. It didn't come out that I was afraid he was going to kill me. I was covered in bruises and my lip was cut. How bad did my injuries have to be?' When the jury's decision was announced, Tom was found not guilty of rape, Eileen decided that she would be better off dead. 'I left the court that day and I just didn't see the point of going on, except that I knew how bad my family would take it. My father said afterwards that what had happened to me was worse than having a death in the family. The policeman who took the case told me that he went home after it and vomited, he was so upset.'

Some months after the court case Eileen attempted to rebuild her life. 'I got a new job and moved to a new area. Then one night, about a month back, I was drawing the curtains in my flat and I spotted a man sitting in a car outside. It was Tom. For a few minutes I just froze. I couldn't move. I ran in to the girl in the flat next door and asked her would she go out and phone my sister, because there's no phone in our house. My sister came down and said that we'd go to the local police-station. Tom followed us in his car the whole way and just parked behind us when he got there. The police said that there was nothing they could do, because he hadn't touched me. If I had been married to him I could have applied for a barring order, but since I wasn't married they couldn't do anything. He knows where all of my family live so I couldn't go to stay with them. I went to stay with a friend and a few days later along with her and my sister I went back to my flat and moved all my stuff out. The girl next door told me that he'd called in and that he'd left a message. He'd said to her, 'Tell her when she comes back, I'll be back, I'll be waiting for her.'

Afraid to go into work, Eileen has now given up her job and spends her nights sleeping on a friend's sofa. 'My parents wouldn't be able to deal with him, and my sister works during the day. So if I went to her place I'd be on my own and he'd know where to find me. I'm just waiting, not knowing what's going to happen to me. I can understand now why women stay with violent husbands. Not knowing what they will do to you after you leave is so bad.' The only other alternative for Eileen is to emigrate, but she doesn't think that England would be far enough away. Her mental state is such that she finds it difficult to think beyond her immediate need to stay hidden. 'I know that he's just waiting and that he knows I'll have to come out some time. I spoke with his probation officer and he said, 'He doesn't believe that he raped you because he was found not guilty.'

If she had a choice again, Eileen does not believe that she would go to court. Her whole life has changed because of what has happened to her and she doesn't believe that it will ever be the same again. 'After so many years of being terrorised you can't really live your own life. I wonder what he will do to me this time and will I come out alive. Years ago I was so different. I went wherever I wanted and did what I wanted. I'm not the same person that I was before. I don't have any confidence. Now it's like I'm in a trance. I can still see every moment of what happened that day. Any little noise I hear at night, I'm awake wondering if it's him. If he had been found guilty it would have given me a chance to get away. There are still days when I think of doing away with myself, but then I think about my family. I would be better off being locked up somewhere; at least then I'd be safe.'

According to Olive Braiden, director of the Dublin Rape Crisis Centre, for a rape victim who goes to court the 'healing process' does not really begin until the court case is over. 'The woman has been waiting for this time to fully recover, so she's effectively on edge the whole time. Then there's a big anti-climax, whether the assailant gets off or not. If he's sentenced there's vindication of some sort, but if he's acquitted or gets a suspended sentence it feels as though it's all been a total waste of time. Society is saying to this woman, what happened to you is not really important.' The way in which the case is conducted by the prosecution can also have a strong effect on the victim. 'The whole procedure, where the case is not being fought as much as being presented, makes it seem as though all of the work is being done on the defence side. 'The Judges have information on the defendant but not on the victim. Occasionally they will ask for some information on the victim. From our point of view we are seeing it from the side of the woman, that she has right on her side. She's looking for vindication; she does it so that she won't let him get away with it. The legal system on the other hand is saying, if there's any doubt, then we have to let him go free. In their direction to the jury, Judges say how important it is that they make up their own minds and they tell them how serious it is to commit someone to prison wrongfully. Everything in court is about the defendant.' In the aftermath of court cases, Olive Braiden and her colleagues have often seen victims having to change houses and jobs. 'We've had schoolgirls who've had to change schools and who are afraid to go out in the evening. Nothing like that ever happens to the accused. We still hold that the only way the whole procedure of going to court will be improved for women, is if the woman is entitled to have her own legal representation. With every flawed judgement it becomes clearer and clearer that this is needed.'

Although changes have occurred in the law surrounding rape, from the point of view of the rape crisis centres it still is not enough. Olive Braiden points to the 'date-rape' scenario as one in which definite views about male and female sexuality are coming to the surface. 'Once there is foreplay involved it is seen as though there is consent. This feeds into the idea that men can't control themselves, that they can't stop. That's insulting to all men. If a girl or woman decides that she doesn't want to have sex, she can say no at any time; men have to understand that no means no. If men can take pleasure from having sexual intercourse with somebody who doesn't want to have sex with them, what does that say about them?'

Despite people's increased awareness of the trauma of rape for the victim, there are very few victims who do not feel guilty or partly responsible for what has happened to them. Rape crisis counsellors admit that the client who comes in to them and actually feels angry about what has been done to her is one of a very small minority. For the woman who is walking home and is raped by a stranger guilt comes in the form of wondering why she chose that particular route, why she didn't manage to get away, what was it about *her* that singled her out for attack? For the 80 per cent of rape victims who know the person who raped them there is the guilt of wondering why the person they trusted did this to them. Should they have been more friendly/less friendly in order to avoid attack? Should they have seen some sort of warning signals?

Joan White, a psychologist and counsellor with the Dublin Rape Crisis Centre, lists the primary emotions a woman goes through in the first few days after she has been attacked. 'The first thing she will feel is shock, then there's disbelief and then a complete reorganisation of everything she ever believed in, not just her feelings towards men, but in general her self-esteem just plummets.' Anger is not usually the first emotion a victim will feel, Joan White says, but rather, 'She will feel pain, hurt and bewilderment. She will ask "why did this happen to me; what did I do wrong?" Very few women come to a rape crisis centre who have not had guilt. The proportion who are angry is very very tiny. Most women find it hard to face up to the fact that somebody can just take away the sense that one is in charge of one's own destiny. How her family and friends react to what happened is also very important. If she is not received well that can also be a devastating trauma. Very often the victim believes that she is going to die. Very often her assailant has said, "I'm going to kill you." Like anybody who's had a near-death experience there's a complete reassesment of one's life. She may wonder if she will ever feel normal again. If the person knows the assailant it's very hard to make sense of it at all. If you think that you haven't made a good judgement in trusting somebody you wonder if you will ever be able to trust anybody again.'

There are other issues that the victim will confront, the primary one being her attitude towards her own body. 'It usually takes some time before she begins to wonder about her sexuality and what effect the assault will have on future relationships. Above all, the victim will worry about being assaulted again. The fears that will surface will centre around "Will he get me again?" I wouldn't feel that I could say confidently to a woman not to worry about that, because the fact is that it does happen. The other thing is that, as anybody who's been the subject of a physical assault will tell you, your whole nervous system is afraid. In much the same way as your body can tense up before someone attacks you, it can remain tense afterwards.'

When the assailant is known to the woman, issues of alliance come up for other people, which will also affect the victim. 'If he's a member of the family, the family may divide into different sides, and if he is a member of the community some people will team up on his side, and this is very difficult for the woman who has to go on living in that community.' What happens immediately after a rape is crucial. Since the victim is sensitive to the least remark everything is highlighted. 'If the woman isn't free to tell what happened to her, recovery is much, much slower. If a woman has had to bury what happened to her it will come up again. The number of calls we've had since the Lavinia Kerwick case shows that. We've had middle-aged and elderly women who were raped as young women and were never able to find anybody they could talk to.'

When a friend of hers told 'Anne' that this book was being written she phoned and asked if her story could be included. 'I am one of the women who didn't report what happened to me to the police, and I didn't go to a rape crisis centre at the time. I never felt that I had the right to.' Anne was raped at the age of seventeen by one of her brother's best friends. Later while studying law at university she suffered a nervous breakdown which she now attributes to the rape. 'I bottled it all up for so long that one day in the middle of a lecture I just snapped. I was too frightened to get up from my seat. I felt that everybody in the room knew what had happened to me.' Anne did not tell her family about the assault nor did she tell any of her friends until some years afterwards. 'I suppose I felt that I was in some way responsible for what happened. I felt that he would get me if he heard that I had been talking about it. To meet him you would say that he was a very quiet, almost shy, person. That's why I had liked him when he called in to see my brother. I met him one night when I was in a pub with my friends and he was on his own. We had a drink together and we were getting on fairly well. When he offered me a lift home it seemed a natural thing to accept it. He lived near me and he was someone I knew and trusted. He stopped at a building site on the way home and said he was running in there because he couldn't wait to go home to use the toilet. When he came back he came round to my side of the car. I thought that he'd just made a mistake and I was actually laughing at him when he opened the door and dragged me out. I could not believe that this was the same person. There was no warning or anything. He was calling me all kinds of names and saying that he knew what I was like. All I could think of was that he was going to kill me. I was screaming and shouting and he put his hands around my neck. He told me that if I didn't stop he would finish me off.'

After he raped her Anne's assailant told her to get back into the car and said that he would drive her home. 'That was one of the reasons I didn't tell people afterwards. How could I explain to them that I had got back into the car with him? But I just wanted to keep him calm and to get home. Outside my house he said that if I went to the police he would say that I had asked him to drive me to the building-site and that no one would believe me. He said that I had been flirting with him all night and that I'd want to watch myself in future, that that is what happened to girls like me.' When she got home Anne did not wake anybody up to tell them what had occurred; instead she stayed in bed for a couple of days and said that she had a sore throat. 'A couple of weeks later he called round to the house, as if nothing had happened. I just locked myself in the bathroom. The awful thing was, I felt like he had some power over me. I nearly wanted to say to him that I wasn't going to tell anybody, in case he tried to do anything else to me.' Later that summer Anne's brother emigrated to America. On a number of occasions, after she started college, she saw the man who attacked her in some of the pubs she normally went to. 'If I saw him in a particular pub I would stop going there for weeks until I felt that it was safe again. Then I had the breakdown and I left college for a year and went back after that and finished my degree. I went for counselling and that was the first time it came out. Once I'd told the counsellor I felt that I could tell a few close friends. One of them said to me that she knew someone else that the same guy had attacked, two years after he had attacked me. She never reported it either. That killed me to think that he had done this to me and to her and probably to other women and nothing ever happened to him.'

In her evidence to the Joint Oireachtas Committee on Women's Rights, Anne O'Donnell, then education and information officer with the Dublin Rape Crisis Centre, made the following point in relation to rapists who re-offend. 'Men who sexually violate or sexually abuse have a locus of control problem, and the more they do it, the more they want to do it. In other words, whatever satisfaction they get from the pleasure of getting away with it is intensified each time that they do it ... . The research coming out of other countries indicates that by the time a sexual abuser or a sexually violent man or boy has been detected he will have committed somewhere between thirty and seventy sexual offences. There is a kind of pyramid effect. You cannot presume that when you have 1,000 victims of sexual abuse there are 1,000 offenders. The chances are that there are much fewer offenders. In other words every offender will have committed several crimes and we have evidence of this from our own work in that many of our clients would be victims of the same offender.'

While all of the country's rape crisis centres report that

the numbers of women disclosing sexual assaults of various kinds are increasing yearly, they will also say that not everybody who is raped or sexually assaulted will report it. The number of rapes/sexual assaults reported to the Dublin Rape Crisis Centre has increased from 76 in 1979 (the year when the centre was first opened) to 408 in 1984, rising to 1,479 by 1990. An analysis of the figures for 1990 shows that the vast majority of the victims, 90 per cent, were female, while 10 per cent were male. The majority of callers, 76 per cent, reported instances where a single abuser was involved. However, in one case eight abusers were involved. The most common scene of the abuse or assault was the victim's home. Only 11 per cent of victims had reported the abuse to the police, with eight cases resulting in the conviction of the abuser and three still pending. Pregnancy had resulted from the assault/abuse in 52 cases (4 per cent). Among the women who became pregnant, seventeen were bringing up their child, nine women had placed their baby for adoption and eight women had terminated the pregnancy. In the Clonmel Rape Crisis Centre figures for rapes reported to them in 1991 show that out of 42 rapes only two were reported to the police. At the Limerick Rape Crisis Centre an average of 10 per cent of rape victims would report the assault to the police. Mary Crilly, administrator of Cork Rape Crisis Centre, puts their client average of reporting assaults at a high level of 25 per cent. Of that 25 per cent, however, she reckons that 'only about one-third will eventually get to court. We have had the terrible problem of women coming to us and telling us that they just got a note from the police saying that the case wasn't going ahead. No-one explains to them what has happened or why the DPP's office has decided to drop the case.' The low rate of reporting rape or abuse to the police can be attributed to a number of factors, not least of which is the perception by rape victims in particular that they must prove that they did not 'consent' to what was done to them.

Rape and the law

Up until the 1980s the law on rape in Ireland was governed by the 1861 Offences Against the Person Act. Under the Act, rape was defined as unlawful carnal knowledge against a woman's consent. The maximum sentence applicable was penal servitude for life. As the Dublin Rape Crisis Centre explained in their review of this legislation in 1979, 'Because rape is an offence which by nature is generally carried out in the absence of witnesses, proving that the intercourse which took place amounted to rape is very difficult. The *mens rea* (criminal mind) of the defendant is also of relevance and he may state he believed she consented. Once this state of affairs arises, the woman, in practice, finds herself in a situation where she must prove that she did not consent. Where visible signs of violence or resistance on her part exist, her case can be easier. Evidence that she did not violently resist can be interpreted as proof that she consented (in other crimes such as robbery this would be absurd).' In their interpretation of the 1861 Act the courts traditionally applied a number of criteria when attempting to judge whether a woman consented or not. These included the 'evil' fame or 'good' fame of the victim, whether she 'searched for the party involved afterwards,' if the defendant fled afterwards, and if the place where the rape occurred was such that she could have screamed and could have been heard. Where the woman attempted to conceal what had happened to her, that was deemed to have lessened her case. Rape cases were also ones in which the jury was warned about the danger of convicting without corroborating evidence. Lawyers often quote the famous dictum of Lord Hale with regard to rape cases, 'Never was an accusation so easily made and so hard to be proved, and so harder to be defended by the accused, though he be ever so innocent.'

Under the laws of evidence rape cases were also distinguished from other cases in that the accused could bring up the victim's previous sexual history without losing the protection of the law. Normally if the character of the woman/victim was brought up, the accused was deemed to have 'dropped his shield' and his criminal background could then be brought up if he had one. In their lobbying for change in the 1970s the Dublin Rape Crisis Centre asked that a victim's previous sexual history not be brought up in court except where the Judge deemed it relevant to the woman's relationship to the accused. They also wanted the definition of sexual intercourse to be extended to include forced oral sex, forced anal sex and the use of objects. They asked for the introduction of a fixed date for rape trials and the right of the victim to have someone representing her in court. Though the Criminal Law Rape Act of 1981 updated the law on rape, the points raised by the Dublin Rape Crisis Centre were not all included. Undaunted, the centre began lobbying again, this time for the repeal of this legislation and the inclusion of what they termed 'certain essential areas' in any new legislation. As well as the extension of the definition of the rape and the exclusion of evidence about a woman's previous sexual history they also lobbied for the guaranteed anonymity of the complainant and the criminalisation of rape within marriage. In 1987 the Law Reform Commission (LRC) was asked to review the crime of rape with a view to formulating proposals on reform of the law.

Various groups, including the country's rape crisis centres, legal representatives, women's groups and the police made submissions to the LRC. Although the 1981 Act restricted the way in which a woman's previous sexual history with persons other than the accused could be brought up in court, the LRC noted the rape crisis centres', disquiet with this area. The centres had pointed out that in their experience of court cases, such evidence was often introduced by counsel for the defence without making any formal application to do so. Instead, the woman's character was undermined by means of hints and innuendoes. Dealing with this question the LRC said that if this was happening then it was up to the counsel for the state to bring attention to it. On the issue of consent, the LRC pondered the fact that there was no legal definition of consent and thus it could be open to individual interpretation. Based on definitions which had proved successful in other countries they suggested that 'consent means a consent freely and voluntarily given,' and that 'a failure to offer physical resistance to a sexual assault does not of itself constitute consent to a sexual assault.'

When it came to rape within marriage, the LRC recommended that it be criminalised and said that 'some misgivings were expressed as to whether it might not lead to fabricated complaints and unwarranted intrusions in the marital relationship.' The LRC, while accepting that they had been made aware of the 'isolation felt by many rape complainants and of their common feeling that they are treated as objects rather than persons within the criminal process,' did not see the need for separate legal representation for the victim. Instead they argued that 'simple changes in practices and attitudes' could alleviate the distress felt by the victim. They therefore recommended that the complainant should have some access to her own statement to the police as a matter of course, that she be kept fully aware of developments in the case, and that she be afforded access to prosecuting counsel in advance of her case going to court. In practice, this has meant that the state counsel will usually talk to the victim about five minutes before the case is due to begin. Where the defendant has been aquitted of the charges, victims and their families may be lucky enough to get another five minutes of the state counsel's time as he leaves the court.

The Criminal Law (Rape) Amendment Act of 1990, while it extended the definition of rape, and provided for marital rape, allowed for the plaintiff's previous sexual history in relation to the accused or other men to be brought up in court, at the discretion of the presiding Judge. In practice, as Olive Braiden of the Dublin Rape

Crisis Centre points out, 'if the defence counsel asks for leave to bring up the complainant's previous sexual history, in our experience it is rarely refused. Since most women are raped by someone that they know, it would be rare, if the woman had had a relationship with the accused, for that *not* to be brought up.' Explaining this whole issue when giving evidence to the Joint Oireachtas Committee on Women's Rights on behalf of the Incorporated Law Society, solicitor Michael Staines gave examples where Judges should consider allowing such questions. Quoting a suppositional case mentioned in the criminal law revision committee report he said, 'Where the defence are aware, for instance, that the particular woman involved is a woman who goes to a particular pub every night, chats up complete strangers and brings them back to her flat, makes love to them or has sex with them for a payment of money; if, in fact, the whole case depends on whether she consented to have sex with the accused person, the jury should also be aware of those facts before they come to a decision. Another example may be where a person denies that she consented to have sex with a member of a gang or group and it can be shown that she has had sex with every member of that group quite regularly, this is something that the jury should be made aware of.'

livid rage

Viewed in this light, the legal argument is that when a jury can only depend on the victim's word against the accused, to prove that she did not consent, then anything which might imply consent must be taken into consideration. The fact remains, however, that previous sexual history is used to justify consent in a wide range of circumstances as are a number of other criteria. If for instance the victim has been drinking with the accused then that will always be brought up in court. If she allowed the accused to see her home, that will also be considered significant. One cannot say that these facts should not be brought up, but the weight assigned them often reflects unrealistic attitudes towards women. In the normal course of events women will go to public places, they may drink alcohol and they may allow someone to bring them home. To impute from that, however, that they were consenting to sex reflects the morals of a time when women never ventured out in public unless chaperoned or accompanied by their husband or father.

One leading defence barrister in a consultation with women's groups had no qualms in privately admitting, 'Our job is to get our client off, to give him the best defence we can; if that means smearing the victim then that's what we do.'

The LRC in its report recommended that 'a positive attempt be made to ensure that some court officials or attendants at rape trials are women'. The prospect of telling what happened in the course of an assault can be a daunting experience for all rape victims; to have to do so to a room full of men adds to the trauma. Some rape victims also feel that the number of men and women on a jury may influence the decision which is made. The old standard whereby defence counsel usually tried to ensure that they had an all-male jury in rape cases has changed. One prominent barrister is quoted as saying, 'Where consent is the issue in a rape case, older women will often side with the alleged rapist. The kind of case I mean is where a girl is alleged to have slept with the defendant in the past or where she goes to a dance, meets a man and goes to the mountains or back to his flat. The older woman will say, "She was asking for it." In that case, I'd object to a young swinger being on the jury if I was prosecuting. Men don't necessarily make good jurors from the defendant's point of view. An older man with a daughter could be very anti-man when faced with the details of an alleged assault.'

Dealing with the question of corroboration the LRC came to the conclusion that the warning usually given by Judges in rape cases on the dangers of convicting without corroborating evidence should no longer be mandatory but up to the discretion of the individual Judge. The Criminal Law (Rape) Amendment Act 1990 upheld this recommendation. Shortly after the bill was enacted, however, the Court of Criminal Appeal in a decision given in 1991 put forward the view that 'it may still be desirable in certain cases under new rape legislation for a Judge to exercise his discretion and warn jurors of the hazards of rape convictions based on the uncorroborated evidence of women. The Court of Criminal Appeal advised this course yesterday even though the new legislation does not require a Judge to warn a jury,' according to the report in *The Irish Times*.

Underlying many of the decisions made by courts are rigid views of male and female 'nature'. Not only do lawyers reflect the views of the society they live in, but their training means that they will incline towards the traditional and normally applicable viewpoint. Societal attitudes towards women have undergone massive changes in a short period of time, but that does not mean that such changes will be taken into account by the courts. The idea for instance that it is dangerous to convict a man on a woman's uncorroborated evidence has its origins in the belief that women will make malicious and false accusations of rape. In a research paper presented to the National Council for Civil Liberties in Britain, Polly Patullo pointed out that, 'Those who believe that rape victims lie might look to the report of the New York City Rape Analysis Squad which found that only 2 per cent of rape charges reported were false and that these figures were not out of step with false charges made for other serious crimes.'

Stereotyped views of male and female sexuality also come into play in court decisions on sexual assault charges. The notion of the 'sudden sexual urge', especially as it applies to younger men, is one that may be used by defence counsel if a client is pleading guilty. In one case of indecent assault on a girl who was a slow learner, which went to trial in Dublin in 1991, the presiding Judge said that, 'If this was a case of sudden sexual impulse,' he could 'seriously consider leniency,' but that was not the situation.

The traditional view in rape cases is that a woman's behaviour must not be seen to have a bearing on the case if the assailant is to be found guilty. When questioned in studies carried out in other countries, convicted rapists admit that the reason they pick on a particular woman has nothing to do with her behaviour at the time, but on the fact that she was there. If it had not been this particular victim it would have been another. Many had attempted to attack other women a short time before an assault took place but were disturbed in some way.

While the victim's responsibility for what happened to her comes under close scrutiny, the assailant may not be held as fully responsible for his behaviour. Sudden sexual urges, drink problems, marital problems, financial worries can all be taken into consideration in a plea for leniency. The fact that the defendant pleads guilty also weights the potential sentence in his favour. Various court decisions have held that if a guilty plea is entered on behalf of the accused then that will be taken as a mitigating factor in passing sentence. Opinion differs, however, on how the courts should weigh a guilty plea. An analysis of this particular question appeared in *The Irish Independent* on 17 July, during the course of the Lavinia Kerwick case. 'Some months ago, Mr Justice Paul Carney, a most experienced lawyer, held in a rape case in which there were no aggravating circumstances that the least sentence he could impose was five years. This has also been specified by the courts of criminal appeal in England and New Zealand as the normal sentence for rape. The maximum sentence for rape is penal servitude for life. In the absence of a statutory minimum sentence, the Judge may impose any sentence that he likes. The Supreme Court has held that, save in exceptional circumstances, rape should merit an immediate and substantial custodial sentence.'

Why then are these long custodial sentences not being given? The weight being assigned a guilty plea is excused on the grounds that it saves the victim from having to go through the process of giving evidence. The very reason the giving of this evidence is so traumatic is that the lawyers on the defence side attempt to bully, harass and discredit the witness. One long-time court observer admits, that 'cross-examination is becoming harrowing for everybody; the stuff that is being brought up about the girl, the fact that her underwear would be waved in front of her; the whole thing is very distressing.' So what really happens when a defendant pleads guilty is that he apparently *saves* the court from seeing the victim being further abused, reduced and diminshed by the legal process. This, coupled with the willingness of the court to accept excuses by the defendant for his behaviour relieves the judiciary from the onerous task of examining the root causes of violence against women.

6

Suffer little children

Angela asks to be interviewed at night. She is afraid that a neighbour who knows her husband will tell him that an unknown person has called to the door. 'I'm so afraid of what he would do if he knew that I was telling anyone about this,' she says. Angela met her husband Liam when she was just sixteen. He was a colleague of her father's and his interest in her flattered her, at first. 'The idea of a wedding seemed to take on a momentum of its own. Liam is quite wealthy and my family were really pushing me to get married, even though there was a ten-year age difference. It was like I was being passed from my father to Liam and I had no life in between.'

Within a few months of marriage Angela realised that Liam was not going to change his normal routine for her. 'He was away a lot on business and when he came home he was always out with business friends. I was delighted when I got pregnant but he was angry. He hadn't wanted children and from then on his attitude towards me changed. When our daughter Emma was older he started taking a lot more interest in her; he had no time for small babies.' At the age of four Emma began showing signs of mental and physical disturbance. 'It started off with bed-wetting. Then it became very hard to get her to go to sleep. Even though she loved play-school, suddenly she didn't want to go anymore. She wanted to be with me all the time. I took her to my local doctor, a woman, and she asked me if I ever left Emma with babysitters she didn't like. That was the first time the subject of child abuse came up. When I said this to Liam he became really angry and told me that I had a filthy mind.'

When her daughter's behaviour became worse, Angela brought her to a child psychologist. Based on what Emma disclosed to her, Emma was later validated by other professionals as having been abused by her father. 'I was devastated,' Angela says. 'I went home to my parents, and their reaction was even worse. First, they said that Emma was lying; then, that I had put the ideas in her head and finally they said that if I went further with this I would ruin her life.' After taking legal advice, Angela decided not to take a civil action against her husband. Her solicitor said that Emma was so young, it would be difficult to prove the case in court. Also, at that stage, Emma had become really frightened of her father. 'I had confronted him and he just said I was mad and that he'd have me signed away. He said I wasn't looking after Emma properly and that she was looking for attention and that I'd lose her if we went to court.' Helpless in the face of the opposition of both her family and her husband, Angela did not take any further legal action. 'We separated about six months after that and now Emma is with me. I hate seeing her go to him for visits but what can I do? I'm the one who feels like a criminal for talking about it.'

In 1987 the then attorney-general asked the Law Reform Commission (LRC) to undertake research on the question of law reform in the area of sexual offences, concentrating on rape and the sexual abuse of children. The LRC soon discovered that their brief could not be confined to the narrow area of legal change, but that a number of disciplines had to be called into play when dealing with this subject. In relation to child abuse in particular, the commission found itself taking evidence which defined everything, from the reliability of children as witnesses, to the use of videos in giving evidence, and on to defining what could be termed a family home if a child was not living with her or his parents. Into this equation they placed the various professionals already working in the area, and they also dealt with submissions from groups as disparate as Family Solidarity and the Gay and Lesbian Equality Network. The issue of child sexual abuse had first come to public prominence in Ireland when a multidisciplinary seminar on incest was held by the Irish Association of Social Workers in 1983. Prior to that event, the subject of child abuse had come up twice. On the first occasion, the authors of a supplementary report attached to the final report of the task force on child care services asked that sexual abuse be included in the schedule of offences which would justify compulsory intervention to protect a child. In 1982 the Irish Association of Social Workers at their annual conference had proposed that Department of Health guidelines on non-accidental injury should include sexual abuse.

The issue of the sexual abuse of children had arisen for health professionals in other countries because they found that children were disclosing it in the course of assessment. Ireland followed this pattern, prompting those working with children to come together and pool their resources and information at various conferences. In 1985 the Department of Health set up a working party on child sexual abuse. Its brief was to gather information which could contribute to practices and policies in this area. The first task which the working party set itself was to actually define child sexual abuse. In its broadest definition they saw the term as referring to a range of sexual behaviour involving children, but initiated by older persons. The fact that their research was the first such work meant that they touched on many controversial issues, including the difficulty of determining the actual level of abuse in any particular case.

What the working party was able to draw upon was the experience of other professionals and interviews with incest survivors in order to draw up some kind of victim and abuser profile. In 1984 for example a survey of school counsellors had revealed that counsellors were dealing with an increasing number of adolescents who were experiencing sexual abuse at home. A survey of 1,000 medical practitioners in 1985, of whom 383 returned questionnaires, found that 132 GPs had dealt with 256 cases of child sexual abuse between 1980 and 1985. A survey of fifty-seven County Wicklow GPs in 1983, of whom twenty replied, found that eleven of the twenty had come across incest cases but only three doctors had reported them to the adult or child psychiatric services. In 1985 official police figures began distinguishing between the different age-groups for victims of sexual crimes. These revealed that more people under seventeen were assaulted than adults. The country's various health boards only began distinguishing sexual abuse from other forms of abuse in 1983 and their figures of confirmed sexual abuse jumped dramatically from a total of thirty-three confirmed cases in 1984 to 452 confirmed cases in 1987, reaching 600 in 1990.

One of the biggest myths faced by those working in the area of child sexual abuse is that it is a modern or 'fashionable' phenomenon, and that increased publicity has served only to give otherwise ignorant people 'new ideas'. The falsity of this assumption is best illustrated by the fact that in every Irish rape crisis centre the largest number of clients are adult survivors of child sexual abuse. These range in age from seventeen to seventy, and for many of these men and women, the death of the abuser or the birth of their own children may be the triggers which cause them to seek help. For children who are still at risk, increased openness about abuse has meant that there is some chance for them of outside agencies actually stopping the cycle of abuse. A major handicap to action in this area has been that the paucity of statistics has been used to justify inaction. Unless programmes are properly set in place, then abuse does not come to light in the first place. Both the working party's report and later the report of the LRC pointed out that without mandatory reporting, cases of child sex abuse could be dealt with in an *ad hoc* and inconsistent manner, and that in some cases no investigation would be carried out.

In order to assess the level of abuse in Ireland, the Sanctuary Trust and Radio Teilifís Éireann (RTE) commissioned a pilot survey from the Market Research

Bureau of Ireland (MRBI) in 1987. From a sample of 500 Dublin adults, thirty, or 6 per cent, reported that they had been sexually abused as children. Slightly more females as opposed to males had been abused, seventeen of those abused were working-class, thirteen were middle-class. Less than half of these victims reported the abuse at the time, and one-third never told anybody. The fact that so many of those who reported the abuse were male, in this confidential survey, whereas in general more females are reporting abuse, suggests a phenomenon that many agencies are only now coming to terms with: boys would appear to feel that they are not being encouraged to disclose sexual abuse in the way that girls are. Another difficulty encountered in compiling statistics on abuse is that there is still a reluctance to call in agencies like the police and the health boards because of fears of the punitive effects this might have. When the Sexual Assault Treatment Unit at the Rotunda was dealing with children the number of cases reported to them exceeded the number being reported to the police and the health boards.

In their ground-breaking report on *Child Sexual Abuse* to the Eastern Health Board (EHB) in 1988, presented in 1990, Robbie Gilligan and Kieran McKeown found that 'the effect of increasing numbers of allegations of child sexual abuse by both adults and children has been to increase the demands on health care professionals responsible for the care and protection of children.' In concrete terms, what social workers were saying is that on average one-third of their time is being spent on child sexual abuse cases.

One social worker interviewed for this book, was dealing with fourteen cases which he said were all equally complex and which caused him immense personal worry. 'In one case the child is still with the family but I just don't know how well her mother can protect her. What happens if she just decides to go out to the shop for a minute, leaving her with the abusive parent? Getting an abuser on to a treatment programme is near-nigh impossible, yet, taking the child out of the home punishes the child. If the abusive parent leaves you still have him being allowed access. Even if the access is supervised, who supervises it? We are being stretched to the limit and the resources are just not there to back us up.'

The positive side of the high priority being assigned to child abuse in the late 1980s was the opening of the two child sexual abuse assessment units in 1988 which was welcomed by all of those working on child abuse. Based in the Temple Street and Crumlin Children's Hospitals in Dublin, the new units were funded by the Department of Health. Money was also allocated to the eight health boards to enable them to improve their assessment of child sexual abuse. In the voluntary sector, the Irish Association of Social Workers set up a voluntary telephone helpline, which closed due to lack of funding, and the Sanctuary Trust was also unsuccessful in its bid to open a resource centre for abuse victims and their families. The controversial nature of child abuse has definitely led to a feeling on the part of statutory bodies that they would prefer to fund efforts which come under some sort of official control. The Gilligan and McKeown survey points to the most difficult aspect of child sexual abuse, which is the actual validation of abuse. Of the 990 cases of alleged abuse known to community care teams and surveyed by Gilligan and McKeown in the EHB area in 1988, 52 per cent were assessed as confirmed abuse, 40 per cent as unconfirmed and 5 per cent as confirmed non-abuse. Ninety-one per cent of the cases were discovered through disclosure by the child. Three-quarters of the children whose cases were confirmed were abused more than once, with one-quarter suffering abuse for one to three years. Another quarter were victimised for more than three years. Only 20 per cent of these cases involved civil proceedings.

The Law Reform Commission on child sexual abuse was equally concerned about the fact that the health boards were reluctant to call in the police on cases, if they had not already been involved. In their consultation paper they warned, 'One of the consequences of excluding police from the early stages of investigation is that it may ultimately make it more difficult to mount a successful prosecution against the alleged offender ... . Those charged with the responsibility of caring for children fear the loss of control which comes with the institution of legal proceedings, which appear to take on a life of their own.' What those working on the frontline do agree upon is that an inter-disciplinary approach needs to be taken, and that the inconsistencies must be dealt with in a forthright way.

According to Gilligan and McKeown, 'child sexual abuse cases pose a particular problem for the criminal justice system.' Dealing with children's evidence, handling abuse within a familial situation and carrying out appropriate sentencing are three of the major problems associated with court proceedings. Hardened legal observers admit to being nonplussed at the sentencing handed out in child abuse cases in particular. 'It would appear,' one legal expert admitted, 'as if the rights of adults superseded those of children in these cases. Judges are reluctant to be seen to be breaking up a family.' While comprehensive recommendations were made by the LRC's report in relation to the training of personnel to deal with child protection and even of lawyers working on the issue, only one subsection made reference to Judges. 'Opportunities should be provided for Judges and Justices who may be dealing with child sexual abuse to acquire information by way of training courses and otherwise as to the special problems provided by such cases.' Where the commission did break from the normal legal inhibitions about interfering with the judicial process, and put on record a comment which could equally apply to rape cases, was in relation to cross-examination of child witnesses. 'Under our adversarial legal system it is the duty of a defending lawyer to use every legitimate means to secure the acquittal of his client. Hence he is perfectly entitled to conduct a cross-examination which is designed to unsettle a child witness and reduce his or her credibility as a witness to the lowest possible level. Secondly, in an imperfect world there will always be defending advocates who will seek to harass or bully a child witness in a way which is not only psychologically harmful but may also be damaging to their own client's case.'

'Lucy', a lawyer who has taken a number of civil actions in child sexual abuse cases, points to various anomalies in the way in which the children are treated by the legal process. 'If a case is being taken, then the evidence, including the validations and assessments, has to go to the Director of Public Prosecutions (DPP). I had a child abuse case which involved very dreadful abuse and the parents got on to their local police station. The attitude was that they didn't want to process it. A lot really depends on the attitude of the police. When the children get to court, it's usually the circuit court and it's very intimidating for them. These cases should really be dealt with in the equivalent of a family court. An older child is going to be subjected to fairly intensive cross-examination. That's another hurdle you have to overcome; and with a younger child the lack of corroborative evidence makes a case very hard to prove. With older boys the court's attitude is that it may be experimentation and anyway there is no place to send them if they are convicted. If the perpetrator is elderly or a businessman the view is that prison is no place for him, and he gets a suspended sentence. In state prosecutions if there's a plea of guilty then the Judge is not given the full facts. You get the bare charges and then a whole host of evidence about how wonderful the abuser is, with the local priest and employer giving evidence on the defendant's behalf. The state barristers can be quite a lazy lot at times. A lot depends on the prosecution evidence and sometimes it can be sloppy.'

The despair felt by lawyers like 'Lucy' is echoed by some of the professionals working on child abuse cases. Tales abound of carefully constructed cases being lost by bad court work or a lack of understanding on the part of Judges as to the long-term effect of abuse on a child victim. Children At Risk in Ireland (CARI), is one organisation currently doing follow-up work with child abuse victims. CARI takes children for counselling where abuse has already been confirmed by other agencies. Their listed effects of child abuse on the victim include 'loss of trust, low self-esteem, deep emotional pain, difficulties with sexuality, difficulties in forming relationships.' They also list the 'coping mechanisms' which children may develop, such as 'living a lie, being afraid that if she or he speaks about the abuse the family will be split up, protecting other family members by assuming an adult role. The child is literally robbed of childhood.'

Geraldine McLoughlin, a psychologist with CARI, feels that there is an urgent need for research on the prevalence of child sexual abuse. Since it opened to the public in May 1992 CARI has seen a total of eighty families. 'Our client range in the younger age-group would be from two to twelve, breaking down to a fifty-fifty ratio between boys and girls. Because women are coming out and saying that they were victims of child sexual abuse, girls are picking up the message that it's okay for them to speak out about it. When young girls are in residential care their key workers are also picking up on the signs of sexual abuse, whereas residential care centres for young boys would not be as aware of it. We really need more open discussion by men who've been sexually abused.'

CARI's current caseload is breaking down to 50 per cent intra-familial and 50 per cent extra-familial abuse. 'With extra-familial abuse, the majority of the abusers we are coming across are young boys ranging from nine to eighteen years of age. This is very worrying. Nine times out of ten, cases are being thrown out by the DPP's office, either because they feel that there isn't sufficient evidence or because of the difficulties in taking evidence from a five-year-old. A number of social workers are finding that the police are becoming very frustrated. We're also coming across families where the young guy, who is the abuser, knows that he's gotten off and he taunts the family. The question we must be asking as a society is, what message are we giving to young boys that they feel this is acceptable?'

A dilemma for anyone working to highlight these issues is the notion that no-one can be trusted with children. 'Somebody asked me recently,' Geraldine McLoughlin says, 'were we abolishing all male babysitters, and I said that this is an insulting message to give to our next generation of men. What I would say to those people is, "Ask your children. If your children are uncomfortable with someone, listen to them." We must ask ourselves what message young adolescent boys are getting that a section of them feel it's within their rights to do these things and that this is what men do.' The idea that video nasties are causing the upsurge in young abusers is one that is dismissed by Geraldine McLoughlin. 'Unless we make serious attempts to look at and understand power within relationships, we won't see what child sexual abuse is. It's not an addiction, it's not the result of a dysfunctional family, it's an abuse of power.' Though she acknowledges that there is a link between boys who have been abused going on to abuse others, her experience is that 'a lot of boys who abuse obviously feel that intimidation and bullying is acceptable behaviour. A number of young boys are doing it in gangs; if the victim is six or seven years old, she or he is not going to be able to stand up to them.' The idealisation of the family is a phenomenon that she also feels must be looked at. 'De Valera tried to construct a myth around the harmonious family unit and what it did was to make a number of men believe that they owned women and children within the family context, that they could do what they liked with them. That is the core of many of the debates we're having in this country at present.'

The change in the sexual practices of abusers, noted by those working on adult sexual violence, has also been noted by Geraldine McLoughlin. 'A child can be deeply traumatised by forced oral sex and yet it is difficult to collect evidence on this. I would be fully sympathetic with the work the people in assessment units in Temple Street and Crumlin have to do. Young children will tell what has happened to them only when they feel that they're going to be believed. The age-group that we're very concerned about is the pre-pubescent group, because most sexual abuse is still happening at the ages of nine, ten and eleven. Girls may begin to say this is not what other daddies or brothers do; they may only disclose then what has happened to them. They wonder how someone who loves them can do this to them. We've seen abuse victims who've made a number of suicide attempts.'

Unpublished research carried out on 100 Irish psychiatric patients has shown that out of the 100, 27 per cent spoke of being sexually abused as children. The incidence rate of child abuse is hard to gauge, without comprehensive data. What people like Geraldine McLoughlin can point to is that the numbers of people at all stages of sexual abuse show the desperate need for more information and resources. 'People are saying to us that it may be as high as 20-25 per cent but without the research we don't know what the true level is.' The abuser profile compiled by CARI shows that abuse is not related to class but there are other indicators that abusers may have in common. 'There would be a tendency to have an authoritarian attitude or personality, a feeling that it was okay for them to do what they did. Very few abusers admit that they've done anything, even the people who've been imprisoned. Most children are abused by a male who is known to them. The effect on a child can be devastating because their whole experience of love and trust can be really shattered; there's a feeling of betrayal. The adult abuser will usually pick out the victim and groom them for a period of time, giving the child presents, saying, "You're my favourite girl," things like that. It's extremely manipulative and powerful. With adults who were child abuse victims the greatest resentment and hurt experienced by them is that they weren't believed, and they may have made several attempts to disclose what's happened. It's much better for a child if she or he talks straight away; that happens more often with extra-familial abuse.' Some of the mothers that CARI deal with have been through long and painful court cases and some are still involved in custody procedures. The most difficult issue for them, Geraldine McLoughlin says, is when a parent who is an abuser has access to the child. 'The court may have said that access must be supervised but the practicality of that is that someone other than the mother has to give a commitment to do that. As professionals we would find it distressing if a child was coming here and disclosed to us that the abuse had happened again.'

In terms of abuse by young boys in gangs, CARI have come across the situation where one member of the gang was doing the abusing and forcing the other children to watch and/or hold the victim down. 'The child who has been bullied into doing that is usually the first to admit that something has happened. Some of these young boys feel absolutely shocked by what they've done. Once the abuse of power has been exercised the victim ceases to be a human being in the eyes of the abusers. She or he becomes a non-person. Videos don't start that off; they reinforce the idea that you can objectify someone.' The other question that must be addressed, she says, is that society can collude with young boys and men by not making them feel responsible for their own sexuality. 'It's like we're giving messages to children that they have to be guardians of adults who can't control their urges. In the same way women are held to be the custodians of sexuality and morality. If we continue to give these messages then child sexual abuse will not stop.'

Kieran McGrath, a senior social worker specialising in the area of child sexual abuse, says that it is the experience of social workers that in the overall figures of child sexual abuse, very few end up being prosecuted. 'We would say that of the confirmed cases about 10 per cent actually result in prosecutions.' He attributes the reluctance of people to bring cases to the attention of the police to an unwillingness to prosecute members of one's own family if the abuse is within the family, reluctance in general by people to engage in the legal process, and ignorance of how one can use the legal process. 'Supposing a next-door neighbour abuses a three-year-old child,' McGrath says, 'there's no way that child can go into the witness box, but if the parents make a complaint to the police, the policeman may make a memo of his conversation with the child. That gives the police officer the right to interview the man involved. The case may not result in a prosecution but at least the guy has been interviewed. I'm not saying it's always right in all cases for people to inform the police, but police do need to have proper information. When cases do go to court, very few go without guilty pleas. When they do, the odds are stacked against women and children, particularly against children. The courts are very poor fora in which to discover the truth. They were never meant to deal with subtle problems and certainly were not designed for children. On the one hand the criminal law says a case must be proved beyond all reasonable doubt, whereas the civil law says it must be proved beyond the balance of probability. In child abuse cases the civil law has been criminalised and we are seeing child sexual abuse cases where the same tests are being used for putting a child into care as are used for depriving a man of his liberty and putting him in jail.' For some Judges, he says, the constitutional position of the family is all-important. 'Children have explicit rights under our constitution only as members of families.' For some women and children, the notion that they are not held to be equal in the eyes of the law has been a painful lesson to learn.

Madeleine, the mother of two teenagers, a boy and a girl, and a younger daughter now aged ten, only found out that her husband was abusing her two older children when her eldest child, Deirdre, was thirteen. 'I would never have known,' she says, 'except that I literally caught him at it. I was watching a film on the television and I went upstairs to use the bathroom and I saw a shadow leaving my daughter's room. I went in to check on her and I asked her was everything okay. She said no it wasn't and I pulled down the covers and realised that he had been abusing himself on top of her. When I confronted him he said that everyone in the town was at that sort of thing, but that he was the only one who had been caught. He promised me that he wouldn't do it again. What I didn't realise was that though he didn't touch her after that, he was mentally torturing her, asking her did she know what a penis was and what masturbation was.' Some months later Madeleine discovered that her son was also being abused. 'The worst of it was, neither of them knew about the other, and both my son and daughter thought they were protecting each other.' Confronted again, Madeleine's husband agreed to see a social worker, but at no stage would he admit that what he did was wrong or that he had damaged the children in any way. During this time Madeleine herself was subjected to both mental, physical and sexual violence. 'He used to rape me, using a lot of physical violence. I thought then that I was at least saving the children from him. Then one night he raped me and forced my son to watch. Afterwards he took down our marriage certificate and told my son that it was what allowed him to do what he had done.'

By this stage the situation had become so intolerable that Madeleine asked the three children would they be upset if she took them away. 'I was staying for their sake, but in fact they all wanted to leave. I left one morning and went to the nearest city. I was literally walking around it with the three children for hours, not knowing what I was going to do.' After a number of nights in various shelters, Madeleine found a place in a refuge. 'It was only when we got there that the children really began to talk. My daughter cried for days and then she told me that she was afraid that she was pregnant.'

At this stage of the interview Madeleine broke down. The thought that she had been unable to protect her children has deeply scarred her, as has the knowledge that they were abused for a number of years and were too frightened to tell anyone. Some months after they had left home, Madeleine's husband applied for access to his children and was granted it in the district court. 'The Judge said that a man shouldn't be kept from seeing his children. At that stage there was a full investigation going on into the abuse, but that didn't make any difference. I was very lucky that a woman barrister heard about the case and took an appeal for me to another court, without cost, and the access was overturned.' When the abuse case got to court, Madeleine's husband pleaded guilty and got twelve months in jail. 'It had come out in the course of the investigation that the third child, the youngest, was being abused as well but that never came out in court. I wasn't even told that the case was on. He used to say to me, "If you go to the police about me the most I'll get is three years and then I'll come out and find you." He was wrong. He only got one year.'

In Madeleine's case the decision to go to court was not one that she had taken lightly. 'I wouldn't have gone through with it except that the children wanted to do it. They felt that they needed him to atone in some way for what he had done, that he had to realise that it was wrong. Coming up to the day I remember wondering about the terrible ordeal I was putting the kids through. Afterwards the kids told me that they were quite prepared to testify. But I hadn't a clue what was going on in the court; no-one told me what was happening. It was over in a minute and they never testified. The same day a young boy was charged with sexually abusing a little girl. He got five years. Where is the logic in that?' In the initial stages of bringing a case, Madeleine had gone to a free legal aid solicitor whose attitude was so negative she says she felt completely undermined. No-one seemed to realise, she says, the long-term effect the abuse was having on the children. 'My son used to draw pictures and it would always be of my husband with a dagger in his hand and blood coming out of it. Even when we had moved to a safe place the children would rush home from school every day just to make sure that I was all right.'

For Catherine, whose daughter was sexually abused by her husband, the long-term effects of that abuse began to have a fresh impact when the girl reached her teens. 'She began to realise what had happened to her and to feel different from other girls her age. When the girls in her class were talking about sex she was afraid to say anything in case anyone knew that she had already experienced it.' The abuse had started, Catherine says, when her daughter was a toddler. 'When she got older she would never allow me bath her. She told me later that her father warned her that I was never to see her undressed. She wouldn't even go swimming with me.'

The case against Catherine's husband had an initial hearing but the charges were later dropped by the state. At the hearing Catherine's daughter, then eight years old, was put through a rigorous cross-examination by the defence lawyer. 'She was accused of having made her statement up, of having rehearsed it beforehand. At one stage the Judge actually intervened and reminded the solicitor that he was questioning an eight-year-old. After the case she was really upset that she had told the truth and yet she was accused of being a liar.' No-one ever told Catherine why the charges had been dropped, but later some of the professionals involved in the case said that the Cleveland Enquiry (an official enquiry launched into the validation of child sexual abuse cases in Cleveland, England, at which a number of parents claimed that their children had been unjustly taken into care, suspected to be victims of child sexual abuse) had created such a negative effect on child abuse cases that some were not being pursued.

Catherine's family then said that they would raise the money for her to pursue a civil action on behalf of her daughter. 'My parents were devastated by what had happened. My father broke down and cried after the court case.' Realising what she would have to put her daughter through again, Catherine did not pursue the civil action. 'He doesn't have access and hasn't really pushed for it. He has married again and has a second family. I don't take a penny from him. I wouldn't under the circumstances. My daughter decided to confront him once when she got older. She wanted to know why he had done it and if he realised what he had done to her. But when she actually met him, she froze completely. That has been the hardest part for me, seeing what she's going through as she gets older.'

According to those figures provided in the LRC's consultation paper on child sexual abuse, out of a total 288 child sexual abuse cases on the DPP's file in 1988, eighty-eight were prosecuted. The reasons for non-prosecution are many. Those working in the area assert that the criteria for child abuse cases are higher than many other criminal charges. The DPP's office, conversely, would probably say that it would not be in the public interest to bring such a case to court, with all the publicity that is involved, unless the case itself is watertight. From a legal point of view, the problem with child sexual abuse cases is that so many people are called into play once the case begins. From social workers to the police and on to validation experts, psychiatrists and psychologists, both the prosecution and defence are calling on evidence which will support their point of view. Among the experts involved, giving evidence in such cases is no longer as clear-cut as it used to be. In a research paper presented to the Association of Child Psychiatry and Psychology earlier this year, Kieran McGrath pointed out that 'for many a child-care expert the courtroom has become a place of fear and dread. Not only can they not expect to "win" easily, they shouldn't even assume that they will come away feeling like a "most helpful witness who has given valuable assistance to the court ..." which is the sort of compliment that a Judge might have paid in the past. There is now a perception that child-care professionals operate within a hostile legal climate, and indeed some even feel that a type of "open season" has been declared on them.'

The decision in the case *(D&D) v G* and others has had the most profound impact of any cases heard in the past decade on the issue of child sexual abuse in Ireland. In simple terms the judgement in that particular case held that parents in a court hearing involving the removal of a child must be informed in advance of the hearing of all the evidence that is held against them, particularly in cases of child sexual abuse. Thus if, for instance, there is a video recording of an interview with a child alleging abuse, then the alleged abuser must also be allowed see that video recording in advance of the case.

In another research paper, *Child Sexual Abuse and the Law: a social work perspective*, Kieran McGrath has highlighted some of the difficulties arising out of the *(D&D) v G* decision. 'This case also opened up the law to the practices and standards of the High Court but with the legal infrastructure of the district court to administer it.' The use of video evidence in child sexual abuse cases has posed a number of difficulties. The rationale behind the use of such evidence is best summed up in the LRC's report on child sexual abuse. 'There is universal agreement that it is traumatic for children to give evidence of unpleasant experiences and that it is particularly disturbing when they have been victims of parental abuse and have to confront the abusing parent in court. This leads understandably to a desire to shield them from this experience and to a failure to report and/or prosecute the crime. This in turn encourages further abuse.'

One assumption, that the LRC admitted was deeply embedded in society and reflected in the law, was that children make unreliable witnesses. The oft-quoted remark by Judge Sutcliffe, made when he was summing up a trial in the Old Bailey that 'it is well-known that women in particular and small boys are liable to be untruthful and invent stories,' is unfortunately a maxim which seeps through the judgements in some cases of sexual violence. The LRC said that they were satisfied that this assumption that children were natural liars was erroneous.

Unfortunately, many of the recommendations in the commission's report still have to be implemented. As one child-care expert noted cynically, 'You can judge how good a report is by how long it stays on the shelf and the LRC's report on child sexual abuse is a particularly good one.' The need for children to feel that their abuser will atone for what has been done is one that is stressed by Kieran McGrath. The courts conversely do not have to take evidence about the effect abuse has had on a child once the defendant has pleaded guilty. Frustration with the legal system has led to people taking the law into their own hands, those working on child abuse agree. There is also the problem that child abuse is rarely a once-off situation, yet courts will often release a self-admitted abuser without any guarantee that he is going to receive long-term treatment. Research carried out in Britain among convicted child abusers shows that within therapy they admit to an average of over 300 offences. If the abuser moves out of the neighbourhood he normally lived in, he will literally arrive in a new area with a 'clean slate'.

Therapy with abusers has also uncovered the strong defence mechanisms under which abusers operate. These range from denying that the abuse happened in the first place, to minimising the actual incidence of abuse, to blaming the child for what happened. In one recent Irish court case, the judgement in the case held that the man involved had not initiated the abuse but that he had been led on by a six-year-old child. The fact that an abuser is an adult with adult responsibilities can sometimes be conveniently overlooked. If they are imprisoned, treatment facilities for abusers are minimal in this country. The treatment programme at Dublin's Arbour Hill prison where 100 sex offenders are now held, has been discontinued because some of the staff involved have moved on. There is no great enthusiasm among professionals to work with child abusers. As Kieran McGrath explains, 'Some people will see abusers privately, but most people won't touch them. Abusers have very strong defence mechanisms, they suffer from a personality disorder as opposed to a mental illness, and some of them are obnoxious people. People with personality disorders have too many distortions. They see the world in strange ways. So you're dealing with distortions as opposed to reality. Their defence mechanisms have to be very strong for them to break the social and familial boundaries and do something that they know bloody well is wrong.'

The incest offenders programme run by Dr Art O'Connor at the Central Mental Hospital in Dundrum, since April 1989, is one welcome addition to the treatment of offenders in this country.

Along with a group of other professionals, Kieran McGrath himself has been involved in setting up a one-year treatment programme for adolescent offenders. The motivation behind the programme came from the discovery that of forty-six cases of confirmed abuse involving adolescents in one sexual abuse treatment unit in Dublin, some of the most serious abuse was carried out by adolescents. 'There is a very big need to do something about adolescents from a prevention point of view,' Kieran McGrath says. 'Most adult abusers begin abusing in childhood. Adolescent abusers can be helped because they're not as reinforced or fixated as adults, though they have the same problems as adult abusers. They're very immature, they have low self-esteem, difficulties with impulse control, and are very ignorant about sex, though that in itself doesn't cause the abuse.' The link between videos and sexual violence can in McGrath's estimation be drawn, only 'if the guy already has the characteristics that would make him offend. If he has already started abusing then it will lead to an exacerbation of the abuse.' Although only one of the eight young boys in the programme had been abused as a child, all of the boys said that they had been exposed to pornography, especially pornographic videos. As far as the young boys that Kieran McGrath and his colleagues worked with were concerned, they were very clear about what pornography is. 'They told us that *Playboy* was not pornography, but the pornography they had seen were films that were graphically degrading of men and women. One of the things all of the boys lacked was victim awareness. To be an abuser you have to be able to block out any feelings you have for the victim. The one area a therapist has to keep concentrating on is victim awareness. The thing is, all abusers see themselves as victims, not as abusers'.

The four conditions which need to be in place before abuse occurs are: sexual attraction to children, lack of internal control, lack of external control and access to a child. While treatment may deal with the first two conditions and the legal system the third, actually gaining access to a child depends on the child being unable to reveal what is being done to him or her. The child protection programme now in place in some Irish schools aims to make children aware of their right to say no to abuse, yet it has attracted a great deal of controversy. Those who oppose the programme have the viewpoint that, in itself, it is making children too sexually aware and might even lead them to make false allegations against their parents. Child-care experts on the other hand say that they have a greater problem with children who exhibit all the signs of abuse, including the physical signs, but will not reveal who has been abusing them. The notion that children will make malicious allegations against their parents is particularly insidious. What it doesn't take into account is that even in the most bitter cases of marital breakdown children will remain stubbornly loyal to both parents, and that it is with the greatest difficulty that children will admit to being abused by a parent. Many children only realise that what is being done to them is not normal when they reach puberty. In the meantime they will have been very disturbed about what is happening, but be unable to articulate this disturbance, or they may have been threatened into silence.

The Child Care Act 1991 has been a long time in

incubation, given that it has been ten years since the force in child care was set up in 1981, and still not all provisions of the new Act have come into effect. The right of children and their need for protection has been a contentious issue in a country which has constitutionalised the rights of the foetus. The Child Care Act 1991 attempts to give to children specific rights while at the same time balancing the rights of parents as outlined in the constitution. Under the terms of the Act, health boards will be required to prepare an annual report on the adequacy of child care and family support services available in each area. Those involved in researching child sexual abuse say that there is a reluctance on the part of health boards to pour resources into an area which they feel is a bottomless pit. The ruling *credo* seems to be that if cases are brought to the attention of a health board, they will deal with them, but they are not going to go out looking for them. 'When the minority of cases which do involve legal proceedings come to court the attitude of Judges falls between being either slightly sceptical or being absolutely horrified,' one social worker told me ruefully. Considering that the small number of cases coming before the courts have aroused such strong feelings, what would happen if the number of cases increased? Are we employing a sub-conscious regulating mechanism by ensuring that it is made as difficult as possible for child sexual abuse cases to firstly get to court, and secondly secure a conviction?

7

The need for change

On Monday 5 October 1992 a decision was handed down in Dublin's Central Criminal Court which raised public disquiet about the issue of sentencing in rape and child sexual abuse cases. A twenty-year-old Kildare man who had pleaded guilty to raping his eighteen-month-old half sister had a ten-year suspended sentence imposed on him by Justice O'Hanlon. Outlining the reasoning behind his decision Justice O'Hanlon said that he was taking into account the young man's 'wretched childhood' and 'disturbed upbringing' and reports that had indicated that his victim, his half sister was not likely to suffer any long-lasting trauma. The irony of this reasoning, that the defendant's behaviour was as a direct result of his childhood trauma but that the victim would not be affected in the future by what had happened to her, did not escape Irish women. Women were shocked at the assumptions that were being made about the potential for recovery by young victims of child abuse.

Writing to *The Irish Times* a group of psychiatrists and social workers from the child sexual abuse treatment unit at Temple Street Children's Hospital said, 'Obviously there still exists much confusion and ignorance amongst certain professionals and the general public, regarding the impact of child sexual abuse. The conclusion that vaginal penetration of an eighteen-month-old girl by a trusted adult would not result in any "long-lasting traumas" for the child, in our view, contradicts not only the research findings but also goes completely contrary to the clinical experience of those of us working in this area. The weight of evidence from research studies and from clinical experience clearly supports the view that vaginal penetration of a small child does indeed result in very significant physical and psychological trauma for the child.

Clinical experience has indicated that when abuse occurs at a very early age, such as before the child has the intellectual capacity to understand what is happening, or has the language to express the abuse, then a very serious process involving psychological splitting off of the original experience can occur. In other words the body remembers while the mind forgets. It is this very group of children who are often the most difficult to help. As a number of professionals who work hard to treat child victims of sexual abuse, we would urge the need for further education of all professionals involved in this area regarding the very serious short- and long-term consequences of sexual abuse.'

It is doubtful whether any of the judges now making decisions on the fate of adult and child victims of sexual violence will ever take up the suggestion of further education made in the letter to *The Irish Times*. An important recurring theme, when one examines violence against women and children in Irish society, is the apparently low value assigned women and children in the eyes of the Irish state, legislature and legal system. How else can one explain the failure of successive governments to take on board the demands which have been made by Irish women in relation to sexual violence since the early 1970s? The position of Irish women has never been so grave as it is in 1992. While in the past women could hope for change, slow as it might have been, this decade will be remembered as the decade of the backlash against gains made by women during the seventies and eighties. Despite evidence of the fear that women experience daily, in their homes and on the streets, Irish politicians have failed to answer the needs of women. It is not enough to offer women piecemeal legislation, the effect of which is at times apparently negated in practice.

In late Autumn 1992 Irish voters decided by constitutional referendum whether Irish women would be allowed to leave the country in order to procure an abortion abroad and on the same day a second referendum decided whether Irish women could receive information on abortion. While the third referendum contained a new amendment to the abortion clause, 40.3.3. When the date for a referendum was announced and the possible wordings placed under public scrutiny, women's groups began to react. Outrage was expressed at the fact that the constitutional amendments would outlaw abortions for victims of rape and incest. Maureen Browne of the government-appointed Commission for the Status of Women declared the proposed wording 'disgraceful'. 'It's appalling,' she said, 'that women who have been raped wouldn't be allowed to have an abortion here. It wouldn't be happening if it was men who became pregnant.'

The arguments arising from the referenda on the abortion issue exposes the actual, as opposed to the aspirational, position of women in Irish society. If women cannot be trusted to make decisions regarding their own bodies, how indeed can women be trusted to tell, truthfully, of their experiences in rape or sexual assault cases? Where does the right to bodily integrity begin and end for Irish women? Women's rights are judged to be subordinate to their given role in Irish society. That role is confined to being either mothers, wives or daughters. In any of these roles one thing is certain; women citizens of this state are dealt with differently before the law than their male counterparts. This is highlighted by the importance assigned crimes of violence against women and children. One lawyer with experience in criminal defence had no compunction about admitting the reasoning behind the judiciary's treatment of rape and sexual abuse cases. 'Women think that is is a terrible crime for women and children to be raped and sexually abused. Judges think that it is a terrible crime for men to be accused of rape and child abuse.'

The highlighting of sentencing procedures and the treatment of victims by the courts has led many women to ask what protection is being offered to them by the state. If the state fails to protect women, then what is to stop women from taking the law into their own hands? There has been some mention in the courts of 'summary justice' being dealt out to abusers and rapists, as though real justice can be left to the courts to decide. Yet many Irish women feel that the legal system no longer upholds the rights of Irish women, and when change is suggested that lawyers merely argue about 'how dangerous' change might be, and how some changes might lead to miscarriages of justice. The fact that Irish women live in fear of self-confessed rapists and child abusers is surely already a miscarriage of justice and not a result of the law trying to be even-handed.

The apparent mildness of women's demands is in stark contrast to the level of fear experienced. Everytime a suspended sentence is given, following upon a guilty plea, a very dangerous message is being sent out by the courts. 'Yes,' the message goes, 'you have done something wrong, but not so wrong that it requires the full rigours of the law.' The bottom line is that, despite their protestations to the contrary, it appears that the courts do not see the rape and abuse of women and children as being as important as a man's good name or his personal liberty. It is the victim in such cases who is marginalised and the abuser who remains part of mainstream, acceptable society.

In the face of all of these things, women's demands, and the demands of groups working with women and children, have been getting louder. There has been no call to 'bring back hanging', or for compulsory castration. Even the demands for mandatory sentencing in the wake of the Lavinina Kerwick case were tempered with reason. Treatment of offenders is what is needed. Locking men away for long periods of time will not make women feel any safer, though it is a tempting short-term solution to the problems faced by a woman who is beaten daily by her spouse. Women know that without treatment these men re-emerge and re-offend. *even w/ treatment they do*

What women are looking for is a balancing of the rights of women and children with the rights of men in Irish society. That such an imbalance exists is clear from the evidence given by those whose daily work involves them with the victims of violence. Nowhere are the inequalities more glaring than in the area of domestic violence.

Domestic violence

Domestic violence is not yet, in practice, treated as a crime in Ireland. Women are beaten and if the police are called their role is that of peace maker as opposed to law enforcer. The violent crime becomes invisible when it happens within the home. It is seen as 'domestic' and this means private. The family is sacrosanct and within the family certain rights are assigned Irish men in relation to control over their wives and children. As Pauline Conroy Jackson points out, 'It is our attitudes to women and children, the value we assign women and children and their rights to equal citizenship which must come under scrutiny. Irish society has traditionally seen women and children as under the control of husband and father. The catholic church has reinforced the view that women must be subject to the moral control of their husband and father and that they do not have the rights or the capability to act as independent moral agents.' When Irish society examines attitudes to victims of domestic violence it becomes clear that the violence used by men against their partners is acceptable. If it were not so surely it would be truly criminalised rather than excused. The 'she must have done something to deserve it,' attitude is still very prevalent in modern Irish society. Irish society has moved on from the time when workers were considered the chattels of their employers, but the intimate domestic relationships between men and women do not yet merit such equality of rights.

One of the most harrowing aspects of the work of counsellors in refuges is preparing battered women for court cases. The barring and protection orders which are supposed to protect women from violence are not easily granted. Bruises and cuts can heal, so photographs are taken of women when they enter refuges and doctors' reports are prepared immediately. This does not spare women the humiliation of having their injuries questioned when they do go to court. One woman describes having to show a Judge the current state of her arm in court when he expressed some disbelief about the bruising as shown in the photographs. 'Luckily' for her, her arm was still a deep navy from her wrist to her shoulder.

'We talk of barring orders,' Róisín McDermott of Women's Aid says, 'but the reality is that women living in violent situations are not regarded as emergency situations by our government or by the legal aid service. Many women seeking barring orders face a waiting list of up to nine months to a year before getting an appointment with a legal aid solicitor. If women who fear for their safety are entitled to the full protection of the law why then is such protection available to them only if they have money?' McDermott also enumerates the factors which keep women in violent relationships: 'Fear, poverty, economic dependence, and cultural attitudes which blame the woman and protect the offender. These include a political system which does not prioritise the support services which are badly needed and a judicial system which can, unfortunately, fail to treat the issue with the thoroughness which women would demand. This leaves the victim feeling blamed and abused once again.

'Where are women most unsafe? In their homes. From whom are they most unsafe? Their husbands and partners. Why do women remain unsafe?' Answering this last question Róisín McDermott says that 'one of the reasons why women continue to be and to feel unsafe is because of the silence and stigma surrounding violence in the home. We, as a society, must take responsibility for condoning violence against women.'

Even when barring and protection orders are given there is some difficulty in enforcing them. The police argue that they cannot keep a twenty-four-hour watch on a woman's home to ensure that a barring order is not breached and they rightly point out that the penalties imposed by the courts for such breaches are not drastic enough. The reluctance by the police to intervene in marital disputes is not a phenomenon confined to Ireland. The Home Office Report 107 on domestic violence, the Association of Chief Police Officers in Great Britain, who expressed the view that,

> We are, after all dealing with persons "bound in marriage" and it is important, for a host of reasons, to maintain the unity of the spouses. Precipitate action by the police could aggravate the position to such an extent as to create a worse situation than the one they were summoned to deal with. The "lesser of two evils" principle is often a good guidance in these situations ... . Every effort should be made to re-unite the family.

Thus, when men beat and abuse their women partners, the police take them out of their home for a short period of 'cooling off'. But they rarely arrest the violent abuser. One reason articulated for not charging men who have beaten women partners is that the women may later drop the charges. The evidence of both the Adapt report and the report on the police response to 300 cases of domestic violence carried out by Morgan and Fitzgerald, show that the Irish figures for dropped charges run at about 10 per cent. This 'dropped the charge' figure is no higher than that cited for any other criminal proceeding.

Morgan and Fitzgerald offer an insight into the way domestic violence situations are handled in Ireland. The study showed that women, whether legal wife or common law wife, are the main victims of violence. (Under current legislation women who are deemed common law wives are not entitled to seek barring orders or protection orders. Other legal remedies open to these women are injunctions. This entire section of women are being excluded from availing of the legal protection open to legal wives, however meagre that may be.)

Morgan and Fitzgerald show that in 90 per cent of cases in Dublin and 82.4 per cent of cases outside of Dublin, no barring or protection order was in place. In their handling of the incidents, the authors concluded that the police 'primarily see themselves in some kind of counselling role in relation to domestic violence as opposed to a strictly policing function. Secondly, it is clear that there is a strong feeling among police that many such incidents of violence are most appropriately dealt with by the civil law.'

At the conference 'Women and Safety' held in Dublin on 3 October 1992, the Minister for Justice Pádraig Flynn spoke about compelling wives to give evidence against their husbands in cases of domestic violence, this provision to be contained in the new Criminal Evidence Bill 1992. This is the government's committed response to dealing with the problem of domestic violence. All of the available data shows that when women actually succeed in bringing their husbands to court, they receive little or no support. This issue was not addressed by Minister Flynn.

Women's Aid are demanding that the police must prosecute in cases of domestic violence, precisely because they realise that there are women who may have to continue to live with the men who abuse them until a court case comes up. These women are in no position to file their own claims for assault. But the minister's statement, instead of changing the role of the police in these matters, shows that the woman is seen as some kind of 'accomplice' who must be *compelled* to testify. Yet again responsibility is being dumped back on the victim who may have neither the mental nor physical resources to cope with it.

By blaming the victim Irish society does not have to deal with the fact that it has always tacitly supported the batterer. If it didn't, then the state would prioritise this issue. The demands being made by organisations working with victims of domestic violence are quite clear. Firstly, they demand money for research to estimate the scale of the problem. Then resources must be allocated so that women can leave violent situations. 'There are more refuge spaces available in Belfast than for the whole of Ireland,' Róisín McDermott says.

The police must enter domestic violence situations in a prosecuting as opposed to peace-keeping role. The traditional image of domestic violence, that it is confined to a few problem or dysfunctional lower-income families, is not a true one. The number of middle-class women who ring the Women's Aid helpline and who are dealt with by advice visits (where a woman may call or contact the refuge looking for legal advice on her situation) shows that domestic violence permeates all layers of Irish society. 'When we disbelieve the victim,' says McDermott, 'we ensure that fewer women will break the silence about it.'

In its conclusions, the Adapt report says that:

> women do not seek help when the violence first emerges and only leave the relationship after a long period of time when it becomes clear that the violence is not going to stop. Yet ... women ... emphasise the importance of not staying in a violent relationship and of taking early action. It is not easy however to leave a relationship, even if it is violent. The support which the woman perceives is available to her will play a very great part in her ability to do so. The response of the institutions and service providers has an enormous influence on whether the violence ceases or continues as the woman is likely to stay in the relationship if her experience is that there is no help available.

Culturally all of the signals being given to women in this country are that they must stay in a relationship no matter how bad it is. Marriage cannot be dissolved under the tenets of the catholic church and after the 1986 constitutional referendum on divorce the Irish people reinforced the existing ban on divorce in the Irish constitution. Whatever the arguments used in the campaign to ban divorce, the fact is that, in effect, the absolute ban tells women that any type of marriage is better than divorce. That is the message given to women.

For the minority of women who have tried to leave violent situations, little help has been available. The Free Legal Aid boards have nine-month waiting lists but there has been no rush by the government to upgrade this service. Will we have to wait until a woman on a waiting list dies before something is done? The women now living in fear, some of whom were interviewed for this book, know the answer to that last question. The way in which Irish society is constructed and the manner in which the institutions of this state respond to victims of domestic violence states clearly that the lives of Irish women are indeed dispensable.

Rape and sexual assault

For many Irish women the greatest conflict between their culturally assigned role and the reality of their lives comes up in their fear of rape and sexual assault. On the one hand Irish women are told that they are being 'protected' from the fate of their European and American sisters by the passing of laws designed to limit their freedom. In the 1960s and 1970s Irish women were told to beware the 'contraceptive mentality' and the so-called 'liberal society'. By remaining allied to the institutions of this state, whatever the limitations on personal freedom, they were at least safe from the 'downgrading' of women which had occurred in other countries. When women came together in this country through the women's movement and began to exchange stories of battering and rape, scales began to tumble from a number of eyes. The catholic ethos notwithstanding, women were being raped in marriage and in their homes and on the streets. The only difference between Irish women and their counterparts elsewhere was that to keep the *status quo* intact they were expected not to disclose what had happened to them. Many women who did bring cases to court felt they were disbelieved, ridiculed and accused of being immoral. The greatest lie of all was that only women who departed from certain norms of behaviour were raped and assaulted.

What were these norms? They changed, depending on the circumstances. The state, through the legal system, pointed to its abhorrence of rape by giving it the same sentence as murder: penal servitude for life. By the time the 10 per cent of reported rape cases go to court, minus the ones filtered out by the DPP's office, not all of them seem to deserve the laid down sentence. Defendants in rape cases tend to be different from those found in other cases. Extenuating circumstances or grounds for lenient sentencing can be taken into account if they, for instance, have won football medals, have been employers, good husbands, dutiful sons, suffer from drink problems, emotional problems, gambling addictions, uncontrollable sexual urges. The attempt is made, on the other hand, to portray the victims in rape trials as calculating, naïve, bitter, silly, dishonest, less moral than the 'normal' Irish woman and generally somehow responsible for what has been done to them. By the time a court case is finished, many victims wonder who in fact has been on trial.

It is a fair question and one that goes to the heart of what happens Irish rape victims in the legal process. The fact is that, yes, the victim is on trial. The only difference between the victim and the defendant is that the victim has no legal representation. In bringing a man to court, the victims are throwing down a challenge; they are saying that Irish society does not protect Irish women from being raped.

In other catholic countries women are held to be morally responsible for the actions of men. In Ireland this has a particular resonance. The narrow and joyless way in which women's sexuality is delineated by the Irish catholic church has meant that Irish men have been able to abdicate responsibility, while Irish women carried the burden of all the moral choices. Women have not reaped the benefits of self-determination in the Irish Republic. Instead, the state constructed an ideal view of womanhood, uncomplaining and subordinate. Women who did not fit into this idealised image had two choices: take the boat (emigrate), or shut up. In the 1930s, 1940s and 1950s women emigrated at an extraordinary rate from the new state. How many of these were rape and abuse victims whose life did not fit in with de Valera's view of the 'comely maidens at the cross roads?'

The right of a woman to her sexuality is at the heart of the way rape and assault victims are treated in Ireland. 'Rape is a terrible crime,' Mary Crilly of Cork Rape Crisis

Centre says. 'Yet in Ireland it is surrounded by a terrible silence.' Each change in Irish rape law has been painstakingly fought for by Irish women. The idea that these legal changes might also have changed attitudes has been completely undermined by recent sentencing in rape cases.

When the assailant is acquitted or gets a suspended sentence, Olive Braiden, Director of the Dublin Rape Crisis Centre says, 'Society is saying to this woman, "what happened to you is not really important." ' The way in which a case is conducted by the prosecution is very important for the victim. In the Irish case, Olive Braiden illustrates, 'the whole procedure where the case is not fought, as much as presented, makes it seem as though all of the work is being done on the defence side. The Judges have information on the defendant but not on the victim. The legal system says "if there is any doubt, then we have to let him go free." In their direction to the jury, Judges normally advise them in rape cases that they beware of convicting on the uncorroborated evidence of women. Though that has now been left to the Judge's discretion the Court of Criminal Appeal recently advised that 'it might still be desirable in certain cases under the new rape legislation for Judges to advise jurors of the hazards of convicting on the uncorroborated evidence of women.' The fact that such 'hazards' are more an example of attitudes to women in our society and views about women's capacity for 'lying' and 'fantasising' will not be contained in a Judge's direction to the jury. Lawyers talk about balance and the rights of the accused, yet they would balk if Irish Judges instructed juries to 'leave their prejudices about Irish women and their sexuality to one side and deal only with the facts of the case'. Each suspended sentence, each negative comment on the behaviour of the victim, as opposed to that of the defendant, strikes a chord with Irish women. It seems to be saying that the really serious event happening in the court is that a man is being accused of rape.

When the Minister for Justice announced a number of important changes in the Criminal Justice Bill of 1992, *The Irish Independent* analysed these changes. 'As a result of the public outcry over the Lavinia Kerwick case,' wrote Tom Brady, 'the Criminal Justice Bill now contains a number of provisions relating to the treatment of victims of violence. The DPP will now be able to lodge an appeal with the Court of Criminal Appeal against a decision that is considered to be too lenient. Courts will also be obliged to take into account the effects of the crime on the victim before passing sentence. The Minister said that this provision was particularly important where the accused pleaded guilty, as in most cases the victim did not give evidence which would indicate the medium- or long-term effects of the crime. And the courts will have the power to order offenders to pay compensation for any resulting personal injury or loss.'

The new provisions were barely announced when the legal fraternity began to sift through it for anomalies. If the state prosecutor were to look for leave to appeal a sentence then that would change the whole nature of prosecution in this country. State prosecutors, traditionally, present a case as opposed to vigorously pursuing a conviction.

Reports on the victim raise the question of who will make these reports and how detailed will they be? Who will ask for the reports to be presented? Will this provision as usual be left up to the Judge's discretion? Rape crisis centres have been adamant in all of their submissions to government that separate legal representation must be allowed for rape victims. This, they argue, is the only way in which women will be saved from finding themselves, instead of the defendant, on trial. Arguing this point, the Limerick Rape Crisis Centre submits that 'most of our clients who have been complainants in court cases have reported how stressful they found the proceedings to be. They have felt totally alone and unrepresented in the witness box. They have not felt any sense of being protected from humiliating and highly personal cross-examination about their sexual behaviour and general character. They feel as if it is they who are on trial throughout the court proceedings. We recommend that in the interests of justice for all parties complainants of rape or sexual assault should automatically and in all cases be granted state funding to employ their own legal representation.'

What the Limerick Rape Crisis Centre is saying is that the victim must be put back into the legal process. Until now, this has not happened. The omission of this has allowed Judges to make decisions without any reference to what happens the victim or her family afterwards. The victim should also be aware of what is being done on her case throughout the legal procedures and if the DPP decides not to prosecute she should be told why not. The very fact that rape crisis centres, the main group dealing with the truama of the victim, are underfunded is a glaring example of the lack of importance which the state attaches to the victim's experience. Funding must be allocated to enable rape crisis centres to operate and to allow them to carry out the research and eduation which is vitally necessary if women's safety from violence is to be guaranteed.

Child abuse

Under the Criminal Evidence Bill 1992, children and the mentally handicapped will be allowed to testify on a television link-up or through a video recording in cases of physical or sexual abuse. The Incorporated Law Society has urged the Minister for Justice to 'think again' before he brings the new measures into effect. The Incorporated Law Society argues that the combined effect of the new provisions would be to 'make it difficult if not impossible for lawyers representing acccused persons to adequately test the evidence offered by the prosecution'. The Incoporated Law Society, in dealing with the obvious trauma suffered by victims in child abuse cases, suggested that 'as an alternative the witness should attend the court solely to give evidence, and the accused person should be removed from the room at that time. The trial Judge could prevent the defence from hectoring or using trick questions during cross-examination. The intimidating atmosphere of the courtroom would be lessened if the Judge, barrister or solicitor did not wear wigs or gowns.' It is difficult to know, whether the Incoporated Law Society are being particularly single-minded or disingenuous in their defence of accused persons. The 'hectoring' of child witnesses by barristers and laywers has meant that legislation has had to be enacted to protect these self same witnesses from brutal cross-examination.

The Chief Executive of the Irish Society for the Prevention of Cruelty to Children (ISPCC), Cian Ó Tighearnaigh, says that 'the adversarial system often re-victimised and re-abused children, and the main flashpoint for that was cross-examination and the actual appearance in court of the abuser.' Ó Tighearnaigh added that 'a Judge could operate the old system if he thought that it was appropriate. To hear the public statements of the Incoporated Law Society you would think that there were no checks, safeguards, balances or appelate prodecures either within this Act or in the legal system.'

The reluctance of the legal community to change procedures cannot be explained by their fears for the rights of the defendant alone. The changes in the Criminal Evidence Bill 1992 had been recommended by the Law Reform Commission on child sexual abuse, a body which had to take into account all of the various interests at play in the area it studied. The fears expressed by the Incoporated Law Society about procedural change include the fact that in a TV link-up a child might be prompted and that witnesses could be coached. In the same breath, however, they are saying that Judges would be able to protect witnesses from hectoring or 'trick questions'. What they are really stating is that the whole nature of child abuse cases will have to be changed.

The recent campaign to stop a prevention programme

on child sexual abuse being launched in Irish schools is a glaring example of this kind of double-think. The organisers of the prevention programme are being accused of 'putting ideas' into children's heads. Parents are becoming fearful that their children will accuse them of abuse as a direct result of the information campaign. Most parents of course support education programmes which may prevent their children from becoming the victims of abuse. But, as evaluators of similar programmes in Canada discovered, 'adults are concerned that talking about assault will make children afraid or anxious.'

The experience of those working on child sexual abuse in Ireland, however, parallels that of their colleagues in other countries; false denials of sexual abuse by children are much more common that false allegations. The difficulties now being ecountered in bringing child sexual abuse cases to court suggest a clawing back by the law of the miniscule progress that had been made in this area. The feeling following the Cleveland investigation in England (where a number of children who had been taken into care following child abuse allegations had to be released) is that parents' rights had been usurped by social workers. It might be more true to say that for a short period the rights of children were gaining a momentum towards equality and that the balance of power was quickly shifted back to the *status quo*.

The most basic mistake made about child sexual abuse is that it has to do with misplaced sexual feelings. Rather it has to do with power, power over the most vulnerable members of our society. Those working on child sexual abuse in Ireland do so in the face of extraordinary indifference. Apart from a brief halcyon period in the mid-1980s when child sexual abuse was the focus of media and thereby government attention, it has now dropped low on the list of health priorities. As long as it was an aberrant behaviour which could be classified under 'other social problems' no great political statement was being made in directing resources to deal with it. When those working on child sexual abuse began to publicise that it could and did happen throughout every level of society, that it was an abuse of power and had a lot to do with how women and children were viewed by our society, then a veil of silence began to be drawn over the issue. Suddenly child sexual abuse did not fit into the 'normal' view of abnormal behaviour. Child abuse was not a sign of dysfunctional families nor of an addiction, but as Geraldine McLouglin a psychologist with CARI explains, 'It is an abuse of power.'

In a society which has a strongly authoritarian view of women and children, such explanations of child sexual abuse are definitely unpalatable. The changes being sought by those working with victims of child sexual abuse depend on one major shift in attitude by Irish society; that is, recognising children as being integral human beings with the same rights and dignity as adults. To make that leap children must no longer be viewed as 'natural liars', and child sexual abuse must be seen not as a modern phenomenon but as one which has deeply traumatised generations of Irish men and women.

For child sexual abuse to end, the cycle of abuse has to be broken. That involves researching the incidence of abuse and putting the recommendations from this research into operation. The increase in young abusers is noted by those working in this area, but treatment programmes are not being set up on an official basis to deal with adolescent abusers. Why did Kieran McGrath and his colleagues have to set up their treatment programme on a voluntary, after normal working hours basis, with no extra pay? Obviously the official attitude is that abuse will be curbed, not at source with the abuser, but at the stage where it is revealed, with the victim. One mother of an abuse victim was definite about what the real offence was in relation to child abuse. 'The crime is not in doing it,' she said. 'The crime seems to be in saying that it happened.' Health boards are reluctant to call in the police into investigations of child sexual abuse and as the LRC pointed out, this 'may make it more difficult to mount a prosecution against an alleged offender.'

The reluctance of health boards to call in the police is mirrored by the reluctance of the DPP's office to prosecute some cases of child sexual abuse, and the attitude of the courts to those cases which do go to trial. Through its various channels the system filters out cases of child abuse; what could be a deluge narrows to a trickle. As with rape trials, when cases come to court the victim is also on trial. The only difference is that the victim does not have legal representation. The eagerness with which courts seize upon information that the victim has not really been traumatised is matched by their willingness to accept the abuser's excuses. The child's choice in what has happened, especially in the case of a guilty plea, becomes secondary to the fact that, as one observer noted, 'the case is all about what has happened to the defendant.'

Looking for a system which does not penalise the child witness may not seem a very revolutionary request, but it has not been responded to by the legal system. Legal textbooks advise lawyers not to depend on the evidence of children as they are prone to lies and fantasy, and legal practitioners hold this to be a tenet of their practice.

The first and most important development sought by those working with victims of child sexual abuse is that children cannot be excluded from the legal process; their needs and the effect on them of what has happened must be taken into account. Drawing analogies between the way a victim's voice is not heard at child abuse hearings and what happens in other courts, Kieran McGrath points to the Beef Tribunal now underway at Dublin Castle. (While examining allegations of malpractice in the Irish beef industry, the Beef Tribunal has allowed various interested parties to field legal teams to monitor their clients' interests.) 'It is very interesting to contrast the situation (of children) with that of the current Beef Tribunal where almost daily wrangles occur over whose voice is heard and whose isn't. Our laws and procedures make it perfectly acceptable to summarily exclude and silence children.

Since sexual abuse has very little to do with sex and a great deal to do with power, the challenge to a trial Judge is to conduct the case in a way which can symbolise, for the aggrieved parties, that the balance between abuser and victim has been rectified and their hurt acknowledged. Victims and their loved ones don't need to see the return of hanging and flogging to get catharsis from the legal process. However, they do need to see cases dealt with sensitively and they do need to see atonement in some form.'

Outlining what he and his fellow professionals would like to see happen in courts, Kieran McGrath says that it would help enormously, where an abuser is found guilty, for the courts to ask exactly what treatment the abuser will undergo. It is well worth pondering why Irish courts do not ask this question as a matter of course. Their attitude seems to be that abuse occurs in a once-off situation, that the abuser gives into some kind of 'temptation'. Reports on the victim are not considered necessary if the defendant has pleaded guilty. Yet again, an importance is attached to the, usually, adult male which is not equally felt to be the perogative of his child victim. Where the abuse is extra familial, families find it hard to understand how the abuser can be allowed back into the community. In some cases the abuser may live near a child, may even be in the same school as a child, and may subject him or her to taunts and bullying. Like rape victims, families whose offspring have been the victims of abuse may have to move home and schools.

McGrath says that 'the effects of child sexual abuse aren't always apparent without close examination. The most worrying long-term effect of child sexual abuse may be what is called the damaged goods syndrome which impacts on self-image and self-esteem. This attacks a young person's psychic, spiritual side and its impact runs deep. Anguish of this kind may not be extinguished by even a "successful" court case where the accused gets a severe sentence. Imagine the pain, therefore, of a trial which is perceived to have been mishandled.'

As well as surveying the incidence of abuse, so that the extent of the problem can be understood, what professionals are looking for is that the legal system should become more attuned to the needs of the child victim. She or he must be allowed a voice in legal procedures. The effect of the abuse on them must always be taken into account when passing sentence.

The fact that the sexual abuse of children is an abuse of power has to be recognised by the courts. Victims and their families need to feel that the imbalance has been rectified. In civil cases, though families may have the benefits of expert evidence, this area has become the subject of bitter wrangling with experts being called in on both sides. Also, if a range of abuse including sexual abuse has been uncovered, health boards are finding that if the sexual abuse is not proven then all of the other evidence becomes secondary and the entire case may fall. Actually making an accusation of abuse is so fraught with pitfalls and so open to disbelief by the courts, that some relatives of victims are reluctant to go to court. When a mother, in particular, makes an accusation against the father, her husband, the case is often looked at for the 'malicious' element. There is sometimes the presumption that women will lie in order to extract revenge on men. Given how the system is loaded against them it is surprising that child abuse victims and their relatives ever go to court in the first place. By doing so they are constantly exposing the lie that Irish society is more moral than any other and that the state has the best interests of children at heart. Children, like women, may be sacrificed, as Ursula Barry puts it, 'for the greater good of our moral, legal and social institutions.'

Irish women have seen their bodies become the battleground for unresolved moral questions in Irish society. They have had their right to their sexuality purloined in order to save Irish men from facing up to the responsibility of their own actions. The anger felt by Irish women at present is both overwhelming and perfectly justifiable. Women are saying to the legislature and the courts that without full equal treatment and full protection in practice, before the law women are insulted and angered by the state's decisions.

Lavinia Kerwick does not stand alone.

References

Butler-Sloss, Lady (1988). Report on the enquiry in child abuse in Cleveland. London. HMSO.

Campbell, Bea (1988) *Unofficial Secrets*. London. Virago.

Casey, Maeve (1987). *Domestic violence: the women's perspective*. Dublin. Women's Aid.

Clonmel Rape Crisis Centre (1991). *Annual report*. Clonmel Rape Crisis Centre.

Dublin Rape Crisis Centre (1979-1990). *Annual reports*. Dublin Rape Crisis Centre.

Family Law Journal (April 1990). *(D&D) v G*. Vol VII.

Irish Council for Civil Liberties (1987) Report of the working party on child sexual abuse. Dublin. ICCL.

Joint Oireachtas Committee on Women's Rights (1986). Minutes of Evidence 14 May. Dublin. Government Publications Office.

Law Reform Commission (1988). *Report on Rape*. Dublin. Law Reform Commission.

Law Reform Commission (1990). *Report on Child Sexual Abuse*. Dublin. Law Reform Commission.

McDermott, Róisín (1992). *Violence Against Women in the Home*: Paper presented to the Conference on Women and Safety in Dublin Castle.

McGrath, Kieran (1992) *Examination and cross-examination; survival strategies*: paper given to Association of Child Psychiatry and Psychology conference. Dublin.

McGrath, Kieran (1991). *Child Sexual Abuse and the Law*: Paper presented to the Association of Law teachers annual conference, Galway.

McKeown, Kieran and Gilligan, Robbie (1990). *Child Sexual Abuse in the Eastern Health Board Area*. Dublin. ESRI.

Morgan, Mark and Fitzgerald, Mary (1992). *Gardaí and domestic violence incidents: A profile based on a national sample of investigations*: Paper presented to the Conference on Women and Safety in Dublin Castle.

Palutto, Polly (1978) *Women and the Law*. London. National Council for Civil Liberties.

Policy Research Centre (1992). *Breaking the Silence: Violence in the home*. Limerick. Adapt refuge and Mid-Western Health Board.

Second Chance (1992). *Silent No More: Report on the experience and support needs of women who have left abusive relationships*. Dublin. Combat Poverty and Women's Aid.

Smith, Lorna (1990). *Domestic Violence: Home Office Report 107*. London. British Government Publications.

Task Force on Childcare Services (1980). Final report to the Minister for Health. Dublin. Stationary Office.

Index

141